Terrorism

Terrorism

A Special Kind of Violence

Margaret O. Hyde and

Elizabeth H. Forsyth

G. P. PUTNAM'S SONS

NEW YORK

3   5   7   9   10   8   6   4   2

Library of Congress Cataloging-in-Publication Data
Hyde, Margaret O. (Margaret Oldroyd), 1917–
Terrorism : a special kind of violence / Margaret
O. Hyde and Elizabeth H. Forsyth. p. cm. Reprint.
Originally published: New York : Dodd, Mead, c1987.
Bibliography: p.
Includes index.
Summary: Discusses the phenomenon of terrorism,
its forms, increasing frequency, historical origins,
and political, religious, and psychological aspects.
1. Terrorism—Juvenile literature.   2. Terrorists—
Juvenile literature.   [1. Terrorism,]   I. Forsyth,
Elizabeth Held.   II. Title.   [HV6431.H925
1989] 303.6'25—dc19 88-27323 CIP AC
ISBN 0-399-61240-8

Dedicated to
Benjamin Williams Hyde

Contents

Terrorism

O N E

Terrorism: What Is It?

A BOMB explodes at 2:45 A.M. in the bathroom paneling of room 629 at the Grand Hotel in Brighton, England, killing three women and two men and maiming others. The terrorist who planted the 30-pound time bomb had time to eat his sandwiches on the balcony overlooking the promenade, to check out of the hotel, and plant more bombs behind bathroom cabinets in other hotels. In fact, that first bomb did not explode until October 12, 1984, several weeks after he had left. The terrorist, Patrick Magee, along with two other young men and two young women, planned to murder as many people as possible that week in October by concealing bombs in sixteen hotels at the seaside and in London to call attention to their cause of a united Ireland. By killing a large number of people at random, such as British on holiday, American tourists, babies, or anyone who happened to be in the hotel rooms when the bombs exploded, they could increase awareness of their plight. This group of terrorists was captured before they completed their mission. They were convicted two years later in a trial by jury.

On October 3, 1985, four dark young men boarded the cruise ship *Achille Lauro* at Genoa, Italy, acting like passengers, although they were different in some ways from the average tourist. They brought attache cases aboard, rather unusual luggage for cruise ship passengers, and they ate in their cabins rather than the dining room as the ship sailed for Naples, Syracuse, and Alexandria. At Alexandria, 650 of the 746 passengers disembarked for a side trip of sightseeing that would bring them back to the ship when it reached Port Said. Those who remained included the staff and tourists, fourteen of whom were Americans.

The ship continued to cruise along. On October 7, a waiter noticed the four men cleaning rifles in their cabin. Now, the terrorists were unmasked and they decided to change their plans. The four "tourists" turned into hijackers who took over the ship, controlling the location of passengers as they wished. On the second day of the hijacking, they ordered a group of Americans who were being held below deck to move upstairs. Marilyn Klinghoffer, whose sixty-nine-year-old husband, Leon, had suffered a stroke that left him partially paralyzed, tried to wheel her husband toward the staircase. She was stopped by the terrorists, who forced her and her group to an upper deck without him.

After the group had left, the terrorists wheeled Leon Klinghoffer toward the ship's rail. There, one of them shot him in the forehead. In order to dispose of him, they went back to the dining area where some passengers were being held, ordered two of them to go on deck and to throw Klinghoffer and his wheelchair overboard. The splash may have been heard by Mrs. Klinghoffer and others on the deck above.

By this time, news of the hijacking had reached shore, and there were threats and rumors. Bit by bit, the horrible truth leaked out.

On October 9, the terrorists agreed to swap their hostage passengers for a promise of safe conduct to a secret destination. When the ship sailed into port, the staff of the ship and the remaining passengers were still suffering from the shock and horror, but the four gunmen were laughing. About thirty-six hours after the hijackers were taken off the *Achille Lauro,* they were put aboard an Egyptian airliner for a flight out of the country. In a bold interception of the Egyptian jet, the United States Navy ordered the plane to land at the American Sigonella Air Base in Sicily.

The fate of the hijackers was left to the Italians, and after a trial in the summer of 1986, sentences were passed. Some of those involved, those who masterminded the original plan, were sentenced in absentia.

In the days and months that followed, terrorists continued to strike, and the coverage of their acts continued to be extensive. The subject of terrorism holds a special fascination. Even though far more people are killed crossing the street than are killed by terrorists, terrorism is widely discussed in personal conversations, the media, and in government. The amount of damage and the number of people killed by terrorists is very small when compared with ordinary crime, but terrorists' acts are often of great political consequence. Some experts are concerned about the possibility of more sophisticated terrorism that could become a fundamental threat.

Opinions about the importance of terrorism vary. Some experts feel that it should be kept more in perspective, while others consider it a major security threat that affects lifestyles of both public officials and private citizens. No one is immune from the threat.

While it is generally agreed among terrorism experts that America is the prime target of terrorists today, the very definition of terrorism remains obscure. What is terrorism?

A young man is arrested when his backpack is searched at a border crossing. He claims that he was delivering a package for a friend and had put it in his backpack with his shirts and jeans without opening it. He claims that he had no idea that the box contained 17 pounds of plastic explosive (which is enough to make several car bombs or demolish a small building). Can one prove that he is a potential terrorist?

Farmers in Minnesota gather to do violence at a forced farm sale. In Nebraska, a farmer fights off at gunpoint the men who try to serve him with civil papers concerning a debt. The Ku Klux Klan's violent attacks on blacks and civil rights workers are well known. Are these and similar incidents examples of terrorism?

The question, What is terrorism? has many answers, for terrorism is easier to describe than to define. Terrorism goes back in history to the time when people learned that others could be influenced by intimidation, but the seeds of modern terrorism were not planted until the last few decades.

Terrorism's record is long and bloody, and modern terrorism is increasingly violent and destructive. The arrows, daggers, and gunpowder of old have been replaced with new, powerful weapons that are easily available. Terrorists no longer have to throw their bombs. They can drop them in wastebaskets or send them through the mail and be far from the scene when the explosion takes place. Hand grenades, automatic rifles, a few pounds of plastic explosives are readily obtainable. A hand-held rocket that is only four feet long and can be dismantled so that it can be carried in a suitcase fires a heat-seeking missile that can down an airplane at landing or takeoff. Today, terrorist attacks can kill and injure large numbers of individuals at one time. Today, no country is blameless.

In an age of increasing terrorism, the same questions are asked again and again: "What can and what should be done to prevent further terrorism or to counterattack? Who are the terrorists? Is terrorism a form of warfare beyond nuclear? Where will it lead? Just what is terrorism?"

When people talk about terrorism, they do not always mean the same kind of action. Definitions of terrorism are difficult and imprecise, but almost everyone considers the following recent acts as terrorism.

The April, 1986, bombing of La Belle disco in Berlin, Germany, that took the lives of two American servicemen and a Turkish woman and wounded more than 200 people, including dozens of off-duty American soldiers will remain in history as the terrorist act that provoked the bombing of Libyan military installations by United States planes on April 15, 1986.

The hijacking on June 14, 1985, of a TWA airliner by Lebanese Shi'ite Muslims on its flight from Athens to Rome resulted in the death of one American. Over a hundred Americans were held hostage for a total of seventeen days.

The hijacking of the *Achille Lauro* cruise ship in October, 1985, and the killing of a sixty-nine-year-old American in a wheelchair aroused intense emotion against terrorists.

The killing of 18 people in the Rome and Vienna airports by Arab gunmen on December 27, 1985, was an important terrorist move that aroused governments to search for new methods of counterattack.

The attack on American ships in international waters by Libyans in the Gulf of Sidra on March 24, 1986, was considered a terrorist act by the West, while the presence of the ships was considered a terrorist act by Libyan leader Qadaffi.

The air strike by United States planes on five Libyan military installations at 2:00 A.M. Libyan time on April 15, 1986, was cited as self-defense under the United Nations Charter against a state for the sponsorship of terrorism. The attack was quick and decisive, but some innocent people were killed. While this killing was not deliberate, the strike caused much controversy.

Although terrorism is difficult to define, attempts at definition help to give a better picture of the subject. The 1986 Vice-President's Task Force on Combating Terrorism spent several days trying to agree on a definition and selected the following: "The unlawful use or threat of violence against persons or property to further political or social objectives. It is usually intended to intimidate or coerce a government, individuals, or groups or to modify their behavior or politics."

Terrorism has been called a disease of modern society, a condition of life, a science, an art, an unsurpassed weapon of psychological warfare, the ugliest word in the English language, undeclared warfare, and the antithesis of democracy and the democratic spirit. Some observers believe that World War III has already begun in the form of terrorism.

According to the Rand Corporation, sponsors of considerable research on the subject, terrorism is violence, or the threat of violence, calculated to create an atmosphere of fear and alarm. It is often directed against innocent targets, and the acts are intended to produce effects beyond the immediate physical damage they cause. It is an act of the weak against the strong.

Terrorism has been classified in many ways. When the cause is sponsored by an established country for a political goal, it is known as *state terrorism.* When the cause is for ethnic autonomy, as in the case of Basque separatists, the terrorism is known as *separatist-revolutionary.* When the action is sheer revenge against a country for real or imagined injustice, the terrorism is *revolutionary.*

All terrorism is criminal, but terrorism differs from ordinary crime. Criminals pursue personal gain, while terrorists act for psychological reasons, seeking to frighten and/or destroy, in order to pursue a cause.

Terrorism has been called a fight for liberty, vigilantism, anarchism, guerrilla warfare, and many other names. By most definitions, terrorism actually differs from some of these, for it technically includes actions that are psychological, that seek to frighten others to publicize a cause such as repression of dissent, revolution, and national liberation. There may be short-term objectives such as freeing comrades from prison, seizing ammunition, embarrassing government authorities, robbing banks, and obtaining ransoms for further operations.

Most terrorists carry out their acts in large population centers. Guerrillas formerly operated mainly in the countryside, developing popular support as they fought, but urban guerrillas have increased recently. Usually, terrorists are an elite group working against the general public. They try to achieve their goals through provoking the government to embark on the course of action they desire, and hopefully enlist the support of the people, which is the next step toward revolutionary guerrilla warfare. While journalists often include guerrilla warfare as a form of terrorism, some authorities insist that guerrillas are not terrorists but irregular soldiers who wage war on military forces, not on civilians. Terrorists are not freedom fighters, even though they are often considered to be. Freedom fighters do not consider women and children fair game to further their cause. Terrorists are oftentimes indiscriminate killers, and their violence is deliberate, not mindless.

As acts of terrorism spread at an alarming rate, it becomes clear that the problem affects the political, economic, and social stability of the world. Although the actions of many terrorists appear to be localized, there are groups that are supported by countries, many of which are built on the foundations of Marxism and Islam. These groups take action abroad to such a degree that many authorities are pleading for acknowledgment by Western democracies of a state of war existing between them and certain terrorist-sponsoring nations. Others are pressing in the direction of keeping terrorism in perspective.

Some fairly firm conclusions have been drawn by Western intelligence over the past few decades, according to Rushworth M. Kidder, a staff writer for the *Christian Science Monitor*. Libya, a country that has reaped large amounts of money from its oil industry, is known to have supplied millions of dollars to terrorist groups. The USSR is believed to have funneled vast quantities of money through eastern Europe to Syria, South Yemen, North Korea, Cuba, and Nicaragua, enabling terrorists to buy weapons for activities in other countries. Some state sponsors of terrorism provide arms directly. For example, five tons of weapons from Libya that were intended for IRA (Irish Republican Army) terrorists were captured off the coast of Ireland. In 1985–86, the United States was found to have been selling arms covertly to Iran and other countries that support terrorism.

Terrorists get support from countries that sponsor terrorism in many different ways. For example, there are "safe houses" and embassies available when they need a place to hide. Numerous training camps for terrorists are believed to exist in Syria, Syrian-controlled Lebanon, Libya, Nicaragua, and Iran. Young recruits are trained in weaponry, methods of assassination, paramilitary tactics, and intelligence gathering. Although state-supported terrorist activities are hard to prove, it is believed that there is a hierarchy among the countries that sponsor terrorism. There is no formal international conspiracy; terrorists are not members of one large global organization, but there are links between terrorists in various parts of the world.

The following example is just one of many in which a number of groups that share ideologies cooperated with each other. In May, 1972, three members of the Japanese Red Army Faction fired on deplaning passengers and bystanders in Tel Aviv, Israel, killing 26 people and wounding 80 people. Palestinians had hired three Japanese, soldiers of the Red Army Faction of Japan who consider themselves members of an international army of terrorism, as paid assassins. The terrorists flew to Israel along with their potential victims aboard an Air France plane from Rome that carried people who were planning to visit the Holy Land. A Puerto Rican survivor is reported to have asked why Japanese kill Puerto Ricans because Arabs hate Israelis. The answer was that the Arabs hired the Japanese terrorists because they could enter Israel without suspicion. The Puerto Ricans just happened to be there.

In the summer of 1985, when Air India Flight 122 disappeared from the radar screen at Shannon Airport, it probably exploded. Bodies and parts of the plane were located in the sea beneath the area where the plane had dropped like a stone. Investigators suspect Sikh terrorists had planted a bomb in a suitcase aboard the plane.

Within an hour of the disappearance of Air India Flight 122, another terrorist incident occurred far across the world. Canadian Pacific Flight 003 from Vancouver, Canada, arrived at Tokyo airport early and passengers deplaned. While baggage was being unloaded, an explosion killed two people. If the plane had not arrived ahead of schedule, it might have been blown from the sky. During the same week, a 10-pound bomb that had been planted in a suitcase killed three people, two of them children, in Frankfurt, Germany,'s Rhein-Main airport. People asked if three separate groups of terrorists were at work or were they somehow connected? Was this timing an aspect of the war being waged by modern terrorists?

Although the capitalist system is a target that terrorists seek to destroy, some terrorist groups have become big business. Their leaders have office staffs, elaborate homes, Swiss bank accounts, and even retirement funds. The men and women under them perform the violent acts. Young men and women in search of adventure or ready to give up their lives for a cause are available to train in their camps and carry out their work. According to James Adams, author of *The Financing of Terror: The PLO, IRA, Red Brigades, M-19 and Their Money Supply*, international terrorists spend a billion dollars a year to wreak havoc. He says the PLO (Palestinian Liberation Organization) has an annual income of between $1.25 and $5 billion.

The rise of terrorism has had a steady and escalating pattern. About ten years ago, the world experienced approximately ten terrorist acts a week. In 1986, the average was about ten a day. The climate of fear increases. From the traveler who fears the indiscriminate spray of bullets in a foreign airport to the people who live in a land that has been battered by terrorists for a period of years, helplessness against possible death is a common anxiety.

Many different types of terrorism coexist, and they range from individual to international. Even definitions of the types of terrorism differ. Generally, state terrorism is recognized as acts of terror by governments such as the terror in Nazi Germany, the use of widespread violence in some Latin-American governments, and the killing of 20,000 Islamic fundamentalists by Syrian troops in Hama in 1982. Domestic or revolutionary terrorists fight against their government. Nationalists, or separatists, fight for their own homeland, and state-sponsored terrorists attack third-party interests on foreign soil. These kinds of terrorism are discussed more fully in later chapters.

Terrorist actions often begin with legal forms of dissent and escalate to sabotage, bombings, kidnapping and assassinations of individuals, and mass murder. There have been warnings about the possibility of terrorists using nuclear, chemical, and/or bacteriological materials. But some experts believe that the increase of terrorism since the beginning of the nuclear age is due in part to states resorting to terrorism as a form of warfare by proxy. This avoids the risk of nuclear war.

Accepting terrorism as commonplace is considered one of the most dangerous trends in the development of terrorism. There may be no greater threat to peace than terrorism and the sequence of events that it can set in motion. In the past, acts of terrorism have played key roles in changing the course of history, and it appears that they will continue to do so. The bottom line is that terrorism works and there is no end in sight.

T W O

Roots of State and Revolutionary Terrorism

TERRORISM is as old as history, but the first great waves of terrorism in modern Europe appeared in France and Russia. France was the scene of state terrorism, a kind in which the terror comes from the government. In Russia, anarchists and revolutionaries fought to overthrow the state.

The tyranny of fear and the terror policy employed in revolutionary France in the eighteenth century stand as a landmark. The French Revolution, which began in 1789, climaxed in the era known as the Reign of Terror in 1793–1794. By invoking the "good of the people," Maximilien Robespierre and his followers rose to power in a society in which all kinds of suspected enemies were eliminated through the use of the guillotine. Robespierre is credited with the beginning of a new kind of terrorism in which systematic violence and threats of violence were used to control opponents and enhance power.

Robespierre is quoted as saying that the mainspring of popular government in time of revolution is both virtue and terror. Without virtue, terror is evil and without terror, virtue is helpless. Although many people considered his theories to be idealistic, others believe that he was a demented man. He believed that terror was justified as a means of helping the people survive their enemies and as a path to their welfare. The government was purified by the axe. Anyone who disagreed with Robespierre's idea of a "moral republic" was sent to jail or to the guillotine.

Although there is disagreement about the time when the Reign of Terror actually began, the fact that it was a bloody time is accepted by all historians. It may have begun as far back as the storming of the Bastille on July 14, 1789, or it may have begun with the September massacres in the year 1792 in which about 2,000 people lost their lives.

Robespierre's speech at the trial of King Louis XVI was credited with swaying the vote for his death. The king was guillotined on January 21, 1793, and his queen, Marie Antoinette, followed him nine months later. Her death sentence served as a warning to others, helping to instill the fear that was so important to the Reign of Terror.

Robespierre spoke of moral virtue as he dealt out death to the "enemies of the people." He claimed to be restoring virtue, to be saving man from his meanness and criminality through execution. Large numbers of heads rolled from the guillotine, causing fear to paralyze the opposition. No one was secure.

Emissaries, in the name of the government and Robespierre's Committee of Public Safety, had the right to dispense with any trial for certain categories of suspects. Many of Robespierre's supporters believed that there was no such thing as an excess of revolutionary power in the service of the people's well-being, and they sowed ruin and death wherever they went. Sometimes children were jailed along with their accused mothers and fathers. The bodies of some victims were so small that the guillotine crushed heads instead of chopping them off. Anyone was a candidate for death; even the members of the almighty Committee for Public Safety began to fear for their lives. Terror was the order of the day.

By July of 1794, enough men opposed Robespierre to unite against him and cause his downfall. On 10 Thermidor (July 28), Maximilien Robespierre was guillotined. The last heads rolled later in the afternoon on the day of his death, for some prison guards were too busy preparing people for the scaffold to take notice that the Reign of Terror had ended.

Robespierre and the small faction of the Jacobin party who dominated France by violence had coerced a nation of 27 million people into accepting their rule. The number of people who were jailed and killed during the Reign of Terror is unknown, but one scholar believes that as many as 40,000 people died and three million were arrested. With the Reign of Terror in France, state terrorism had come of age.

The beginning of large-scale revolutionary terrorism is illustrated by deeds of nineteenth-century Russians against their leaders. Mikhail Bakunin and Sergei Nechayev were two of the earliest pioneers of revolutionary terrorism and their influence continues today. Bakunin, who was born in 1814, was reportedly author of the famous *Catechism of a Revolutionary* with his student, Nechayev. It describes a terrorist as a dedicated man who has torn himself away from the bonds which tie him to the social order and to the cultivated world with all its laws, moralities, and customs. Night and day, he must have but one thought, one aim—merciless destruction. He must be ready to destroy himself and destroy with his own hands everyone who stands in his way. This revolutionary catechism has inspired many modern terrorists.

Bakunin was an anarchist, one who is opposed to all forms of governmental authority. He saw government as the source of all social evil and described it as criminal. However, he believed that any form of terrorism was justified and that all kinds of violence were sanctified by the revolution. Although Bakunin is considered to be the father of modern anarchism and he was a brilliant orator, he did not organize his followers with any forethought.

When Bakunin's activities made him suspect in the eyes of the tsar's secret police in 1840, he left Russia for western Europe. While there, he aided revolutionaries and, after an arrest in Austria, he was returned to Russia to spend six years as a prisoner in two of the tsar's dungeons where he lost his teeth and good health. After he was transported to Siberia, he made a sensational escape on an American ship, went to Japan, then to America and western Europe where he joined other revolutionaries, including Karl Marx, on whose theories modern communism is based.

Both Marx and Bakunin believed that violent revolution was needed to overthrow capitalism, but Bakunin had no faith in the workers. He placed his high hopes on the peasants, believing that revolutionary influence was strongest in those who had no property and no stake in things as they were. Marx felt that Bakunin's philosophy of anarchistic terrorism was a counterproductive force. Marx argued for political change through revolution, a mass uprising that occurs in accord with specific social and historical conditions. Although Bakunin was disgraced when Marx engineered his expulsion from the Socialist International, a worldwide organization of Socialists, his influence is still strong among the anarchists who live and fight by his credo.

Nechayev, like Bakunin, glorified violence. He is credited with organizing terrorist groups into cells, or small units. Two members of each cell belong to other cells, linking three cells in such a way that only two members know the plans of more than one cell. This protects against any one person knowing a great deal about activities. By this system, a person who is captured and made to talk, would have only a limited amount of information. This organizational structure or some variation of it is used today by terrorist groups. Dostoyevsky's famous novel, *The Possessed,* is based on Nechayev's revolutionary theories and practices. Nechayev died in a Russian prison in 1882 after being tried for ordering the murder of a Moscow student who dared to disagree with him.

Before he died, Nechayev may have played a part in the campaign to kill the tsar from his prison cell through coded letters to other terrorists. At one of their underground meetings in the summer of 1879, a group known as the People's Will passed a solemn resolution to do away with Tsar Alexander II as a top priority. Although he was the most liberal of sovereigns in Russian history, the nation's radicals were not satisfied with his freeing the slaves and other reforms. They were hungry for more. Several attempts had already been made on his life by individuals and small, poorly organized groups before the People's Will passed their resolution.

The manhunt that ended in the assassination of the tsar has been called one of the most remarkable in its inventiveness, stubborness, and duration. The first attempt by the People's Will was planned for the fall of 1879 when Alexander II would be traveling from his vacation in the south to the capital by train. Three caches of dynamite lay ready at widely separated places along the route. The route was changed because of bad weather, so the first spot was missed. The charge at the second place failed to explode when the train passed over it. The third charge did go off, but it exploded under the wrong train, smashing a freight car loaded with fruit.

The next attempt was a carefully planned explosion set off in the basement of the Winter Palace in St. Petersburg by a terrorist, Stepan Khalturin, who managed to have himself hired as a carpenter and cabinetmaker with quarters in the basement of the palace. He collected small quantities of dynamite and smuggled them into his quarters until he had hidden 100 pounds of it in the chest that contained his linen and clothing. He knew the floor plan of the palace and the usual whereabouts of the tsar. One evening in February, 1880, he set off his dynamite in the basement at a time and place that he believed would reach the tsar in the dining room of the palace. But the tsar was delayed by an audience of two visiting German princes. Actually, he would not have been killed even if he had been in the dining room, for the major impact of the explosion was in the guards' room, a room that was on a level between the basement and the dining room. The hundred pounds was not enough to seriously damage Khalturin's target.

The terrorists of the People's Will planned another attack. Andrey Zhelyabov and his lover, Sophia Perovskaya, pretended to be merchants when they rented a shop along the street where the tsar often traveled. They dug a tunnel from their cheese shop to the middle of the street where they would place dynamite that would be exploded as the tsar's carriage passed over it. But these plans were thwarted by the arrest of Zhelyabov. Sophia, in spite of her grief, took over the role of leadership of the terrorists. Fast action was needed because of suspicions by the tsar's police. She arranged to have four men with bombs in readiness along the route that the tsar usually took when returning from watching parades. When the tsar's carriage reached the point at which the first bomb thrower was stationed, the terrorist hurled his explosive between the legs of the horses that pulled the carriage. Two people were killed and several others were injured, but the tsar escaped injury. However, as he walked near the scene of the explosion, another terrorist threw his bomb. This one wounded the tsar critically, and he died in the Winter Palace within an hour. Ignaty Grinevitsky, the assassin, was severely wounded in the explosion, and he died from his wounds in the palace infirmary.

The new tsar, Alexander III, smashed the organization known as the People's Will, but freshly formed groups of revolutionary terrorists appeared on the scene in Russia and in other countries. In the period between 1890 and 1908, bombings and assassinations by anarchists took place in many countries. Bombs were thrown at public buildings, at cafes, and theaters. Assassins took the lives of Empress Elizabeth of Austria-Hungary, President Carnot of France, King Umberto I of Italy, and President McKinley of the United States. Not one of these acts led to the overthrow of a government.

In Russia, in western Europe, and in countries around the world, terrorism has a long history. Secret societies have always played an important part in Chinese history, and many of these engaged in terrorism. The terrorist activities of the Boxers in China were extensive and well known. By 1900, this group slaughtered westernized Chinese indiscriminately, setting fire to houses and kidnapping people. Political terrorism and assassinations were part of the history of Japan, the Middle East, Latin America, and North America. Nazi Germany practiced state terrorism and many communist countries continue to do so.

State-sponsored terrorism is a term that is used for cases in which nations use terrorists to further their own goals beyond the territory in which the terrorism occurs. Libya, Syria, Iran, South Yemen, and Iraq are considered to be major sponsors of terrorism today. State-sponsored terrorism has been called modern terrorism, and some of its roots come from the first large-scale terrorist movement, that of the Russian Populists in the 1800s.

Just a few of the early incidents that have had direct influence on modern terrorism have been mentioned in this chapter. Josef Stalin, Adolf Hitler, and Mao Zedong have been called the greatest terrorists of all time. They governed by state terrorism, using terrorism by their governments against their own people.

Terrorism has existed in every generation and every civilization, but much of today's terrorism has its roots in the writings and deeds of those men of long ago.

T H R E E

Young Terrorists

IN EFFORTS to combat terrorism, many studies have been directed toward finding its causes. Why terrorists do what they do is a question with many answers. Most terrorist organizations begin with students who discuss and write about a revolution or ways to produce change. They agonize for a long time before taking the step into violence. Once an organization becomes known for violent deeds, people who have no qualms about violence join them. But there are some groups in which terrorism is passed down from one generation to the next, especially among those who are fighting for a separate homeland. Such is the case today in Northern Ireland where young Catholics and members of the Irish Republican Army (IRA) continue to wage a campaign against Protestants and British authorities in the north of Ireland. Today, many others, such as Libyans, the Popular Front for the Liberation of

Palestine (PFLP), and Russia's KGB, are believed to be working closely with the separatists through an informal global network. The cause of many of the terrorists has changed through the years, but young Irish children grow up knowing one simple thing: the Catholics and the Protestants hate each other.

Sean was in sixth grade when he followed his brother's coffin to a special plot in the IRA cemetery. His brother had been shot in a bloody fight between the Catholics and the Protestants, part of the violence in a complex scene of nationalist terrorism that is filled with bombings, assassinations, and arson. The men and women who marched to the cemetery with Sean ignored the jeers of the Protestants. Sean watched as his brother's coffin was lowered into the freshly dug grave amidst the tombstones that read MURDERED BY THE BRITISH ARMY. He really did not understand much about the long-standing problem in Northern Ireland, but he did know that he hated all the Protestants. He knew that he would kill many of them before he grew to be his brother's age.

Margaret was doing her Christmas shopping when a car sped past her and men opened fire on the British patrol with submachine guns. Some bullets hit shoppers who were walking along the street. The woman next to Margaret was hit in the head and died instantly. Twenty bombs went off in other parts of the city that same day. The IRA claimed that it would destroy Belfast by Christmas. Margaret vowed she would take an active part in driving the Catholic terrorists out of Ireland. Any Catholic was the enemy.

Psychiatrists who have studied the Irish problem have concluded that not much could be done with a child after he or she finished primary school in Belfast, for by that time attitudes were fixed and Catholics and Protestants saw each other as natural enemies. Although some parents do protest against the terrorism on both sides, others encourage the hatred. Many of the children of Northern Ireland grow up confused, obsessed with hatred and fear, to carry on the terrorism they learned as children.

Today, the Catholics feel persecuted as they struggle in what they consider to be a noble cause, the driving of the "British intruders from their native land." The Protestants of Ulster, who outnumber the Catholics, are fighting to retain a "Protestant state for Protestant people." In spite of the fact that both sides adhere to Christianity, many young and old feel strongly that it is impossible to live with each other. They say that they can never forget or forgive the awful things that the other side has done to them.

The trouble is long-standing. Half a century ago, the Irish poet and playwright Sean O'Casey referred to the Irish in their revolutionary struggle against the British during the years 1919–1920 in these lines from his play, *Shadow of a Gunman:* "They count their bullets instead of the pearls on their rosary; their Ave Maria and the Lord's Prayer are their bursting bombs and the rattling of machine gun fire. Gasoline is their holy water and a house in flames is their mass." While some call the Irish terrorism a religious war, others see it as a class war of wealthy Protestants against poor Catholics.

The city of Belfast has been reduced to little more than rubble by neglect and by thousands of bombs. As night falls, iron curtains drop in front of the display windows of the shops. Wire mesh and steel bars are common and graffitti cover walls.

The roots of the violence go back to antiquity, far beyond the Anglo-Irish Treaty of 1921 in which the six predominantly Protestant counties of Northern Ireland (Ulster) remained part of the United Kingdom of Great Britain. The twenty-six counties in the south of Ireland became the Irish Free State. The Protestants of British and Scotch origins who form a two-to-one majority do not want to be part of Ireland. There are many differences between Ireland and Britain, and it is believed that a great many Catholics do not want Northern Ireland to separate from England. So there is some question as to whether or not the terrorism is really just an effort at liberating the country from British rule. The bloodshed in Northern Ireland continues with the original issues clouded.

Riots and violence continue to flare and many organizations have been formed in the attempt to solve the Irish problem. Terrorism has been the order of the day for many years, claiming about 2,500 lives since 1969, according to official estimates. While many people are working toward a peaceful solution, the hate has not ended. In November of 1985, there was an agreement giving Dublin a voice in governing Northern Ireland, but when the first meeting took place on December 11, 1985, over 1,500 police were mobilized to protect the site where the meeting took place. Fanaticism and hopelessness still exist, and young terrorists may well continue to begin their training as soon as they can throw a brick.

A small but especially interesting group of young terrorists struck in Canada in the 1960s. The religious sect known as the Doukhobors began in Russia in the eighteenth century, and emigrated toward the end of the last century to build their own Utopia in a wilderness area of Canada. They carried on the belief that only the law of God must be followed and the law of man can and must be ignored.

The Doukhobors kept their children from public schools, educating them in their own faith. They insisted on total dedication and unquestioning obedience. Children of an elitist group of Doukhobors known as the Sons of Freedom were brought up to burn and bomb government buildings and even homes of their leaders and their own homes. They knew hate and total obedience. Dr. Frederick J. Hacker states in his book *Crusaders, Criminals, Crazies: Terror and Terrorism in Our Time* that the Sons of Freedom are responsible for more than 1,100 bombings and burnings in the first half of this century.

Some of the Basques of Spain belong to a group known as ETA, whose name means Basque Homeland and Freedom and whose members spawn terrorism in the name of national liberation. These rugged, hard-working people, who want to separate from Spain, teach their children to fight for their heritage. They talk about the lost history of the Basque nation and it is believed that a governing council of older men directs young individuals in their acts of terrorism. Even after the death of Spanish leader Francisco Franco, ETA continued to try to destroy the democracy that replaced him.

Although many of the young Basque terrorists appear to believe they are killing for the sake of the Basque culture, members of the ETA stage operations in France, Belgium, and Nicaragua. They have reportedly been trained in Leba-

non, South Yemen, Cuba, and other countries and have had
financial support from the Soviet Union, Libya, and China.
In some respects, these Basque terrorists have become indis-
tinguishable from "Red commandos" of other countries.

In Sri Lanka (formerly Ceylon), there are five Tamil sepa-
ratist groups whose violence makes headlines from time to
time. The Tamil terrorists in Sri Lanka do not represent the
main body of Tamils, but they share the same goals, the
separation from the Singhalese who govern the country. Most
of the Tamils are Hindu and, with the exception of the
northern and eastern sections of the country, they are in the
minority. Strong feeling between Buddhist Singhalese and
the Tamils erupted into major riots in 1983 and continued
through the years. Young Tamils concentrate on bombings,
blowing up bridges, incapacitating vehicles with rocks and
bombs, and ambush-type killings. The government has been
criticized for indiscriminate reaction to Tamil terrorism through
attacking large segments of the Tamil population.

If the Tamils succeed in separating from the Singhalese,
the latter would be deprived of commercial skills, for many
of the Tamils work on the tea plantations and the Sri Lankan
economy relies heavily on the production of tea. One letter
from a small terrorist group warned that tea for export to the
United States and Great Britain was contaminated with po-
tassium cyanide, but this appeared to be false.

Nearly 80 percent of Sri Lankan fishing has been affected
by the terrorist struggle, for many fishermen will not venture
into the sea where violence is common. More than half of the
country's protein comes from fish. Hatred, paranoia, and
frustration run deep. These feelings are instilled in the chil-

dren of both sides and attempts at solution to the conflict have so far failed.

In Puerto Rico, three post offices were bombed early in 1986 by young separatists who are pressing for Puerto Rican independence from the United States. In South Africa, youthful black radicals escalate the violence and tribal warfare that has been a serious problem in that country for a number of years. They are responding to state terrorism in a much more active way than the generation before them, which was more patient with the inequities of apartheid. Much the same is true with the young who are involved in the complex problems of South America.

Among separatists as well as among other forms of terrorists, the young are in the forefront. The examples cited in this chapter are just a small number of the cases in which the young are being trained for terrorism. Today, education for terrorism is taking place in high schools in Libya where students are being taught courses that will help them defend their land. All Libyan students must take at least two of their 36 hours of weekly classes in military training. This includes hand grenade tossing, machine gun assembly and maintenance, signal and rocket launching. One of three months of summer vacation is spent at military camps for field training. A *New York Times* reporter, Judith Miller, noted that Ali Awarith Secondary School in Tripoli resembles a training camp more than a high school. Rocket launchers on the playground replace playing fields. High schools throughout Libya specialize in different kinds of military training.

Fidel Castro has been operating Cuban training camps since 1961 for young people from many countries. In 1969, a number of camps were opened under the direction of Colonel Vadim Kotchergin of the Russian KGB, making a major commitment by the Soviet Union to the terrorist network.

Young Iranians are training to spread Islam throughout the world in a holy war in which they consider it an honor to die for their faith. Small bits of soil from the tomb of the prophet Hussein, grandson of Mohammed and a revered martyr, are placed in the mouths of children. They are taught that dying in a holy war is an honorable way to reach heaven. Terrorism is honorable in the war against Satan. Some children go to war at a very young age.

A tale that is often repeated helps to illustrate the devotion of the young Iranian terrorists to their cause of spreading Islam and sacrificing themselves in this cause. When a fifteen-year-old was captured by Iraqis in the war between Iran and Iraq, he cried. On being told that his wounds were not serious and he would recover, he cried even harder. When questioned about this sobbing, he explained that he was crying because he did not die. He felt that God did not want him.

Young terrorists are trained in many countries. Some people ask, "Why are their camps different from those that train soldiers and other military personnel in counterterrorist camps?" The difference lies in the very meaning of terrorism. Although hard to define, terrorism involves the willful and calculated choice of violence against innocent people. But in the minds of young terrorists, there are no innocent people.

FOUR

Carlos: International Terrorist

WHEN Italians kidnap other Italians or when Irish blow up other Irish, the terrorism is called *domestic political violence.* However, terrorism is not only becoming increasingly bloody, it is becoming increasingly international with terrorist acts on victims outside their own countries.

On March 15, 1986, an "anti-imperialist symposium" was held in Libya with representatives from far parts of the world. The meeting included Basque ETA, East Germans, radical American Indians, Kanaks from New Caledonia, Moros from the Philippines, and factions of groups from other countries. The West considered the meeting a "terrorists' convention."

Today, a terrorism network reaches around the globe, and many small groups with different causes join with each other and with larger organizations. Right wing, left wing, Red terrorists, black terrorists . . . many terrorist groups are loosely connected in this global network. Their links are increasing, making it possible for small groups with limited resources to undertake serious operations. Groups help each other in numerous ways, including financial support, sophisticated weapons, safe houses, training, and specialized personnel.

The international network of terrorists is usually considered to have begun in the 1960s and 1970s. The famous Tricontinental Congress of 1966 in Cuba was a conference to coordinate terrorism and worldwide revolution. Delegates from 82 countries, including 40 from the USSR, passed resolutions that called for close cooperation among the socialist countries with an objective to devise a "global revolutionary strategy to counter the global strategy of American Imperialism." By the 1970s, terrorism on an international scale had established itself as an important force.

One man, Carlos, whose true name is Ilich Ramirez Sanchez, is often called the first international terrorist. Certainly, he is one of the most famous, for his activities were extensive and the list of his global connections in the terror network is long. He captured the imagination of people who were horrified by his actions but intrigued by his exploits. In the introduction to their book, *The Carlos Connection: A Study in Terrorism,* Christopher Dobson and Ronald Payne say that he is "a star on the world stage. He is the bad man in the black hat surrounded by his henchmen from the Baader-Meinhof Gang [a West German terrorist group], the Japanese Red Army, and the Palestinian groups." The late Palestinian leader, Wadi Haddad, made his bookings and Muammar Qaddafi supplied him with money.

Carlos was born in Venezuela on October 12, 1949, but even as a child he traveled almost continuously around South America and the Caribbean with his mother and brothers, and he learned the languages of the countries he visited. His lawyer father grew rich through real estate ventures, but he was a staunch communist supporter who named his sons after Russians he admired and encouraged Carlos' education as a terrorist. Carlos first trained in Cuba, where among other things he learned the value of making friends with women who would provide him with safe refuge and help in avoiding suspicion. He passed as a South American playboy, and often enjoyed the love of three or four innocent women at the same time. Some of his girls harbored locked bags of explosives in their apartments which they were told not to open. Those who obeyed instructions did not know of the nature of his work.

Not all people who knew Carlos as a playboy liked him. In earlier years, he had his problems even at Lumumba Friendship University in Moscow where he indulged himself in drinking, girls, and "hooliganism." The university has the mission of training students "from underdeveloped countries so that they can return to their homelands to become the nucleus for pro-Soviet activities." Carlos, who was expelled at one point, returned for specialized courses in political indoctrination, sabotage, killer karate, and weaponry. He was well trained in the use of explosives, forging of passports, the use of aliases and safe houses (many of which were made available by the girls mentioned earlier). These were useful in many of his exploits, as was knowledge gained earlier in Cuba in subjects about disguise, map reading, urban guerrilla tactics, forgery, and sabotage. One might think of his educational major as terrorism.

Carlos participated in many terrorist acts through the following years, and there are a few people whose names appear frequently in his story. One, an Algerian known as Antonio Dagos Boudia, or Mohammed Boudia, is credited with initiating much of what is called the "global terrorist network." Boudia was a KGB operative and a recruiter who organized and designed many anti-Israeli actions for the European network of the Popular Front for the Liberation of Palestine (PFLP). He is believed to have been the French operative of the Black September Organization that tried to shock the world into acknowledging the Palestinian cause by the slaughter of eleven members of the Israeli Olympic team at the Munich Olympics in the summer of 1972. Boudia's life ended on June 28, 1973, when he climbed into his blue Renault 16 and settled his weight in the driver's seat. A bomb exploded, blowing the doors from the car and killing him as the nuts and bolts from "shipyard confetti" put holes in the roof. His murder was part of the revenge taken by Israelis after the Munich massacre.

After Boudia's death, Carlos was called from his double life in London as playboy and terrorist to take over the post of chief terrorist of Europe. Boudia's death left Carlos with an international network of terrorist agents on which he built his own complex.

Dr. George Habash, who led the PFLP, and his chief of operations, Wadi Haddad, played major roles in the operations of Carlos, too. Haddad appears to have recruited Carlos, helped with his training, and provided him with funds and agents that enabled him to carry out so much international terrorism. Although Carlos was born in Venezuela, he maintained contact with Palestinians and Russians in his high position in the international terrorist movement.

In spite of his extensive training, Carlos botched his first confirmed act of terrorism a few months after Boudia's death. This was the attempted murder of Joseph Edward Seiff, a popular Zionist who was high on Carlos' hit list. When the butler answered the door of Mr. Seiff's London home on the evening of December 30, 1973, he was greeted by Carlos, who was wearing a hooded parka and a scarf that covered the lower part of his face. Carlos forced the butler to lead him to Mr. Seiff, who was in the first floor bathroom. Carlos fired at him on sight, hitting him full in the face. The bullet hit the victim in such a way that it knocked out two teeth and lodged in the back of his neck. His life was spared, perhaps by the fact that the teeth took some of the force from the bullet. Carlos was not identified as the gunman until two years later when the weapon he used was found with a cache of his other weapons.

Carlos was involved in a large number of terrorist acts after the Seiff incident, giving him no time to work on his hit list. He supervised the Baader-Meinhof Gang, the June 2 Movement, and the Revolutionary Cells for Wadi Haddad. He led a few major terrorist actions himself and directed a long list of them. His work as a leader was considered brilliant by numerous groups, but the French police were unaware of his extensive actions until they found him more or less accidentally.

In their investigation of Michel Moukharbel, who worked

with Carlos in the administration of the network and who kept meticulous accounts of activities, Chief Commissioner Jean Herranz and his assistants in the French antiterrorist squad came across a photo of him with Carlos. Moukharbel insisted that Carlos was a small fish in the operations, and there was no reason to suspect otherwise. However, the investigators decided to visit the flat where Moukharbel said Carlos might be on the evening of June 27, 1975. They had no intention of arresting anyone; they went to the apartment for a chat with Carlos. Moukharbel felt certain that Carlos would not be there, and even if he was, the police would only see him as a South American playboy living with a few hippie-type French university girls.

After socializing for a short time at the party in progress at the apartment, the police decided to confront Carlos about his association with Moukharbel. While Herranz went to the door to call Moukharbel, who had remained outside, Carlos went to the bathroom where he grabbed the gun he had hidden in his toilet bag. As Moukharbel entered the room, Carlos believed that his comrade in terror had betrayed him. Carlos fired two shots at him, three more at the inspectors, and still another at Moukharbel. He rushed toward the door and escaped over the balcony.

Moukharbel's accurate records were invaluable to the police, and it was through them that they learned about the women whom Carlos used, the explosives he kept in their apartments, and most importantly, some extent of his activities. The close links between international terrorist networks and the espionage services of some countries were documented.

Carlos laid low for a while. However, when he led the raid on the oil ministers and their delegations at the biannual conference of Organization of Petroleum Exporting Countries (OPEC) in Vienna on Sunday, December 21, 1975, he was the most wanted and most famous terrorist in the world. He used his reputation in his negotiations with the Austrian government.

Carlos' colleagues prepared the ground for his team before Carlos arrived in Vienna, so on the morning of the raid at OPEC headquarters, everything went smoothly. Five men and a woman entered the building with their Adidas bags full of weapons rather than sports equipment, and they soon used their guns. Three security men were shot as they moved toward the conference room, although this was later described as a matter of psychology rather than of necessity. Soon, there was madness in the air as shots were being fired and victims panicked. Carlos, in his beret and raincoat, remained in command of the situation. People in the conference room hid behind the sofa and under the conference table.

One attempt was made to wrench Carlos' weapon from him but Carlos quickly shot the man who tried to disarm him in the shoulder and then pumped three more rounds into him. Only one of the terrorists was wounded in the incident, and after a short battle with the SWAT team that arrived to try to rescue the victims, the terrorists had 71 hostages firmly in their hands.

The prepared communique giving the demands of the terrorists was read and negotiations were soon underway. The Austrians met the demands by supplying a bus to the airport and a plane to carry Carlos, his team, and the hostages wherever Carlos demanded. In Algeria, where the hostages were freed, Carlos is believed to have made a deal for the lives of two hostages whom he had orders to kill, an action that probably infuriated Haddad and Habash. He is reported to have received a large sum of money, perhaps as much as five million dollars, from an undisclosed source for this bargain.

Saudi Arabian Sheikh Yamani, one of the men Carlos was supposed to kill, talked with him while he was a hostage, and he later expressed an opinion that Carlos was interested in the Palestinian cause only as a way of spreading international revolution.

Carlos has been described as the perfect terrorist, who probably only worked for the money. Certainly, after the Vienna raid, he retreated into obscurity, perhaps because he was an embarrassment to his own group, he was tired of terrorism, and/or wealthy enough to retire. Although Carlos disappeared from the scene in 1976, state-sponsored, or state-supported, terrorism grew and new leaders have taken his place. They are part of today's mysterious web of global terrorism.

FIVE

The Bloody Web

MANY names appear in reports of terrorist acts again and again, while other groups spring up suddenly and disappear after just one terrorist act. All are guided by hatred and a passion for revenge, but sometimes names are just a cover for a group that does not want to claim responsibility, for security or diplomatic reasons. For example, the groups known as Islamic Holy War, Organization of the Oppressed on Earth, and Organization of Revolutionary Justice were listed in the *New York Times* of April 28, 1986, as having unknown leaders and numbers of members. They were identified only as Shi'ite groups in Lebanon. Many permanent groups appear to use a special name for a single terrorist act, making it difficult to trace the real leaders. So, in many cases, the real smoking gun remains behind the scene.

In efforts to understand the bloody web of terrorism and

ways to prevent further carnage, some of the key actors and the way they operate are being studied carefully. Small groups are often hired to carry out specific acts by countries that sponsor terrorism. Sometimes clues to such operations are obtained from individuals who are captured during or after the act. Many of these individuals pose as students while they gather information that can be used in an attack.

Each of a number of individuals may be hired to perform a very small task by highly professional organizations so that if one is apprehended, he or she can provide little information about the whole plan. In some cases, two terrorist acts occur almost simultaneously, as in the case of the bombings at Rome and Vienna airports in December of 1985. The small terrorist squads that are probably recruited by the same leader may have little connection beforehand.

Some terrorist acts appear to be carried out to serve a number of purposes. For example, the hijacking of the *Achille Lauro* cruise ship in October of 1985 may have been part of a plot to kill Jews and to embarrass Yasir Arafat, leader of the Palestinian Liberation Organization (PLO) at a time when he might have been considering negotiations with Israel. No one knows the full story of this incident, but it was reportedly masterminded by Abul Abbas, whose personal message had been broadcast to the world in a number of ways. He warned that all Americans are fair targets for terrorist attacks, and that the United States would soon be confronted directly.

Abul Abbas is a young, third-generation Palestinian fighting for a homeland. He is angry with moderate Arabs as well as with the United States and Israel. While some Palestinian, Libyan, Lebanese, and other groups are fighting Israel and the United States, they are also fighting all Arabs who support Israel's existence. Abul Abbas belongs in this category. His rage is fed by memories of humiliations suffered by his people, and although many of his terrorist coups went amiss, he is viewed as a hero by many Arabs.

Many terrorists, such as Carlos and Abul Abbas, seem to be in the terror business willing to work for anyone. Even many of the groups that support specific causes appear to be increasing their links. Gayle Rivers, a New Zealand counter-terrorist, suggests that we think of terrorism as "a universal plague in which the wanton killers of all nationalities have linked arms against their common enemy: the rest of us."

The fanaticism that many terrorists share is difficult to understand, especially by people unfamiliar with their culture. This seems especially true in the case of the Shi'ite Muslims of Iran who are waging a Holy War with the goal of spreading Islam throughout the world.

Most of the Middle East Muslims we know are Sunnis, people who are somewhat Westernized. Most Americans are totally unfamiliar with those Muslims who are hostile to the twentieth-century world and Western civilization. Only a small minority of Muslims have turned to terrorism, but these are fanatical in their beliefs and their motivation to spread the Islamic Republic.

In order to understand the background of Muslim terrorists who are fighting a Holy War, or Jihad, one needs to know something of the background of their religion. Muslims belong to many sects and live in many parts of the world. Muslims of all sects profess the same beliefs, utter the same prayers, and turn their eyes toward the holy city, but there

are some major differences among the sects. They are all followers of Islam, the youngest of the great universal religions.
Islam honors Allah, a single, all-powerful God who spoke
through the prophet, Mohammed. His sayings are preserved
in the Koran, the sacred scripture.

Islam is an Arabic word meaning surrender, or commis-
sion, and those who follow Islam commit themselves into the
hands of Allah. Each believer is guided in his every act by
the word of Allah. Basically, Islam is a noble religion that
demands five principal acts of faith: faith in Allah, prayer five
times a day, almsgiving, keeping the fast of Ramadan to
commemorate the month in which Mohammed received his
revelations, and making a *hadj,* or pilgimage to Mecca, at
least once in a lifetime.

About one-sixth of the world's population is Muslim, the
majority of whom are concentrated in a belt of countries on
both sides of the equator. The greatest concentration of Muslims is in the Indian subcontinent in the countries of Pakistan, Bangladesh, and India, but Muslims are found in small
numbers just about everywhere in the world.

Although there have been thousands of different sects, there
are two main groups, the Shi'ites and the Sunnis. The origin
of these groups lies in controversy over leadership after the
death of Mohammed. Part of the religious tradition empha-
sized by Shi'ites includes what is known as the passion motif,
the origin of which lies in the martyrdom of leaders. Hussein,
the grandson of Mohammed, represents man's struggle against
tyranny, and each year since his death in the seventh century,
the events at Karbala where he and his followers were mas-
sacred are reenacted. It is the duty of these Muslims to carry

on the struggle toward a classless society and abolish all forms of capitalism. Each year, in celebration of Hussein's martyrdom, the Shi'ites fly black flags and hold meetings where they listen to stories about the tragic death of martyrs. They conduct processions that exhibit symbols of slain heroes, and participants in the processions beat their chests with clenched fists, cut themselves with knives, and torture themselves in other ways. The leaders, whom they honor in this way, are considered to be just people who suffered for their righteousness at the hands of heartless enemies.

The very word, assassin, comes from the name of the famous Muslim sect, the Assassins, who appeared in Persia and Syria in the eleventh century. This sect of Shi'ites warred against the Sunni, believing they had a religious duty to kill the unrighteous. The Assassins lived by a strict code of secrecy, using terror to force local political authorities to cooperate with them. They also used propaganda to spread their beliefs to the people, much as terrorists do today. Although this group did not succeed in doing away with the Sunnis, they are credited with setting a model for terrorists in later years.

There has been a wide renewal of consciousness of identity among today's Muslims in a number of parts of the world. Some are noted for educational and missionary activity. In Iran, the Shah attempted to modernize his country, but he repressed dissidents, including religious leaders known as *ayatollahs* (signs of God). The Ayatollah Ruhollah Khomeini was exiled first to Iraq and then to France, but he continued to send his pronouncements to Teheran where the recordings of them played an important role in 1978 and 1979. Street riots and civil unrest based on the revival of fundamentalism played a major role in the overthrow of the Shah of Iran. Certainly, he was not overthrown by conventional arms, but by a liberation movement that was a purifying process designed to free Iran from non-Islamic influence. The roots of the movement came from within, reorienting everyday life around the teachings of Islam. In addition to ridding themselves of foreign influence, the fundamentalists are writing new constitutions, and restructuring tax systems to make them less exploitive. The individual Muslim is offered new direction in all the problems of life through the solutions in the Koran. Islam dictates all facets of their everyday lives, and Islam gives the people hope.

The Ayatollah Khomeini emerged from a life of devotion and humility, away from all materialism and with a willingness to die for the faith. He advocated the use of terrorist tactics to root out Western influence and ideas from the Middle East and to spread his own brand of fundamentalism. The opponents of Khomeini claim that he is using the holy war to distract people from the failure of domestic policies and to preserve his own position. Other ayatollahs dare not speak out for fear of punishment, and it has been reported that the Khomeini regime is responsible for driving between two and three million people into exile, killing 50,000 and imprisoning 140,000 people.

Certainly, Khomeini's contribution to the rise of terrorism is noteworthy. In the holy city of Qom, some 2,000 terrorists from more than twenty Islamic countries have received tactical training, according to a recent report that was prepared for the United States Senate's Judiciary Committee.

Part of the daily language of Khomeini supporters is "America is the Great Satan. America is corrupt. America is a hollow drum. America can't do a damn thing." Nations such as Kuwait, Saudi Arabia, Bahrain, and the United Arab Emirates remain very much at risk from Iranian terrorist surrogates seeking to destabilize their governments or overthrow them outright, according to a recent statement prepared by Nathan M. Adams, senior editor of *Reader's Digest,* for a Congressional hearing. Iranian-sponsored violence and attempts at destabilization have taken place as far away as Egypt, Tunisia, Morocco, Malaysia, Thailand, and the Philippines, Iran spends millions of dollars each year to spread propaganda that supports its fundamentalist revolution worldwide.

Recent reports indicate the possibility of connection between the Islamic revolution and the Palestinian terrorist groups. The Palestinian-Israeli hostility and the Arab-Israeli problem in general is one that is both long-standing and laced with terrorist acts. From the mid-thirties to 1948, extremists on both sides committed terrorist atrocities against each other and against the British occupiers of Palestine.

The birth of the state of Israel on May 14, 1948, was consistent with a United Nations resolution that recommended the partition of Palestine into the international city of Jerusalem, a Jewish state and an Arab state. On the day after the birth of the new nation, armies from many Arab states tried to drive the Jews into the sea, but they were unsuccessful. Hundreds of thousands of Arabs spread into neighboring Arab countries, and an estimated 600,000 Palestinians live in United Nations-sponsored camps in Syria, Jordan, Lebanon, and other areas. About 1.2 million other

Palestinians live outside the camps in these countries and still others are spread throughout Europe, the Middle East, and the United States.

While the Arabs say that the Palestinians were forced from their homeland at gun point, the Israelis insist that they were incited to leave by other Arab states. Many are said to remain in the camps to pressure world opinion in their efforts to establish a homeland and destroy the existence of Israel. These camps are breeding grounds for Arab terrorists. From here, many *fedayeen,* people willing to sacrifice themselves for the Palestinian cause, are recruited.

Many Palestinian liberation groups have been formed through the years. The Palestinian Liberation Organization (PLO) under the direction of Yasir Arafat consists of many groups of *fedayeen* as well as trade unions, women's groups, and refugee camps. The Popular Front for the Liberation of Palestine (PFLP) began in 1967 under the leadership of George Habash, one whose terrorist activities have been mentioned earlier. By 1974 the PLO condemned air piracy, but the PFLP continued its terrorism and splinter groups committed numerous gruesome acts.

An actor in the world of terrorism who vies for fame with Carlos and Abul Abbas is Sabry al Banna, whose code name is Abu Nidal. He broke from Arafat in 1974 and has led a group of terrorists whose actions are directed against Americans and other Westerners, and against pro-Arafat Palestinians and pro-American Arabs in the Middle East.

Abu Nidal emerged as a shadowy figure who has become famous for his violent acts in the murky world of international terrorism. His organization appears to be tightly compartmentalized, and although small, its accomplishments are large. He is believed to have been born in Jaffa to an affluent family and attended French and Islamic schools. Accounts of what happened to Abu Nidal next vary, but he is believed to have adopted the code name Abu Nidal in the mid-1960s when he was a member of Arafat's Al Fatah organization. By the time Al Fatah began to limit its involvement with international terrorism, Abu Nidal was increasing his terrorist activities. After breaking with Arafat, he operated out of Syria, Iraq, and Libya. He was strongly involved in transnational terrorism, changing sides from time to time. For example, he tried to kill the Syrian foreign minister in 1976, but operated out of Syria for some years after that.

Abu Nidal is famous for his statement to the German magazine, *Der Spiegel;* "I can assure you of one thing. If we have the chance to inflict the slightest harm to Americans, we will not hesitate to do it. In the months and years to come, Americans will think of us." He is also famous for his part in the leadership of Black September, a group that sent a hit team to Munich during the Olympics to kill Israeli athletes, and the incidents at the airports in Rome and Vienna in December, 1985. The 1986 hijacking of a Pan American World Airways airliner in Karachi, Pakistan, and the attack on an Istanbul synagogue, both of which resulted in the deaths of innocent victims, may also have been the work of Abu Nidal.

Various Arab states have backed Abu Nidal from time to time, even though he has "sentenced Arafat to death" and considers peace-seekers as traitors. He has murdered a number of PLO representatives in various countries. According to counterterrorist Gayle Rivers, his hate is cast in stone. According to Aaron Miller, a member of the United States State Department's planning staff, Abu Nidal's politics are those of revenge and revolution on a grand scale. In an article in the *Washington Post* of March 30, 1986, Miller suggests that more terrorists like Abu Nidal will follow.

One of the most famous actors in the bloody web of terrorism is Libya's Qaddafi, who seems to bring together many of the terrorist causes. He is described as believing himself to be a prophet of Islam and a mighty creator of a Great Arab Nation. His foreign policy is based on terrorism and he is generous in his financial support of terrorists, in providing them with a safe haven and training. He appears to be obsessed with eliminating Israel and, along with Khomeini, he regards the United States as evil and the ultimate enemy.

Qaddafi has published a *Green Book* in which he outlines his self-taught philosophy. This has been described as a combination of Islamic zeal and Bedouin socialism. He has been called a madman, a manic depressive, an irrational mystic, a vain actor in the web of terror who seeks revenge, and a sick man possessed of the devil. His ruthless support of terrorism led to the United States controversial strike on Libyan bases in April, 1986. Qaddafi played his terrorist game on a smaller scale in the months after the American raid.

The web of terror will continue long after leaders such as Abu Nidal, Abul Abbas, Carlos, and Qaddafi have left the scene. Some terrorists are obsessed with violence; many have an intense hatred of the democratic process. Whether the aim of terrorists is a worldwide Marxist revolution, the spread of Islam, or support for some other cause, it will continue. Palestinians have established links with terrorist groups in Japan, North Korea, Europe, and Latin America. Turks and Iranians and the IRA are connected in the informal network. The individuals of Irish extraction in the United States who supply arms for terrorists in Ireland through NORAID (North American Relief Aid) are linked, consciously or unconsciously, with Libya and Moscow by their support.

Counterterrorists remind us that there are no good terrorists, even though some causes appear to be more to our liking than others. Although some people who are locked into the international terrorist circuit do not realize with whom they are working, others do not care. They are all guilty of supporting indiscriminate murder.

SIX

The Mind of the Terrorist

Ricardo Chavez-Ortiz was a Mexican-American who struggled to support his wife and eight children, working on and off as a short order cook. He had been diagnosed as mentally ill and had experienced several psychotic episodes, but seemed fairly normal in between these periods of illness. One day, he decided to go to Mexico to look for work. From his home in California, he flew to Albuquerque, New Mexico, where he bought a gun and ammunition. The next day he boarded a plane. After takeoff, as he was enjoying the view and feeling relaxed, the flight attendant offered him a drink. At that moment, he suddenly realized what a contrast there was between his situation and the deprivations suffered by Mexican children and others. He decided to do something to help, so he quietly requested the pilot to fly to Los Angeles. He expressed concern over inconveniencing and frightening the passengers, but would not be persuaded to give up his idea. He did not demand anything except a chance to give an address in Spanish on the radio. After the plane landed, he gave a long, somewhat incoherent speech which included pleas for peace and for more opportunities for children. The police then took him into custody with no trouble. Dr. Frederick J. Hacker, an expert on terrorism and the psychiatrist who performed an extensive evaluation, concluded that Ricardo Chavez-Ortiz was confused, delusional, and seriously out of touch with reality.

Dr. Hacker and Dr. David Hubbard, another psychiatrist who has studied many skyjackers, both found from their investigations some striking similarities among the skyjacker terrorists they interviewed. All were very neurotic people, and most were severely disturbed. Most had inadequate personalities, almost all were paranoid, and many were physically weak. They tended to be daydreamers, often fantasizing themselves as powerful and omnipotent. The act of skyjacking usually followed a disappointment in their lives. The psychiatrists theorized that this act was a realization of the fantasy of being all-powerful, and was an effort to counter their feelings of inadequacy.

Many experts in different fields have attempted to identify personality traits specific to terrorists, and to form a profile of the "typical terrorist." Some psychiatrists and psychologists have described terrorists as rigid, unable to make lasting relationships, death-seeking, suffering from underlying depression and feelings of emptiness, and incapable of experiencing pleasure. Many have histories of bed-wetting, fire-setting, and cruelty to animals when they were children. According to these experts, the individual turns to terrorist activities in order to compensate for his deficits, or to overcome his sense of apathy.

President Reagan has referred to Muammar Qaddafi of Libya as a "flake," because of his support of terrorist activity. Many people believe that all terrorists must be mentally ill. However, despite the fact that numerous skyjackers have been diagnosed as mentally disturbed, and despite attempts to find abnormal personality traits in individuals who have carried out terrorist activities, most experts agree that not all terrorists are mentally ill. Terrorism expert Brian M. Jenkins has warned that categorizing all terrorists as mentally ill or impaired appeals to people who would rather not face the fact that the injustices which the terrorists are fighting are real.

Dr. Frederick Hacker has classified terrorists into three groups: the "crazies, the criminals, and the crusaders." Criminal terrorists are those who are neither crazy nor do they pursue their activities for anything but personal gain; they have no altruistic or political goals. The crusaders are those who use terrorist means to further an idealistic cause. Not all terrorists fit precisely into these categories. Some mentally disturbed terrorists may express delusional ideas that involve political themes, and criminals and crusaders may show signs of mental disturbance.

Although researchers have made some useful observations about terrorists, their hypotheses tend to reflect the biases of their particular field, and their theories have been very speculative. One of the problems is that few terrorists have actually been interviewed and studied in depth.

Konrad Kellen, writing for the Rand Corporation, has drawn

some conclusions based directly on autobiographies and actual interviews with several terrorists. Although these individuals differ from each other, they do seem to share some common characteristics.

According to Kellen, turning to terrorism is a gradual process. Many individuals who later become terrorists are young people who feel alienated from society for various reasons—ethnic, social, economic, or psychological.

There are many minority groups in Europe that want to secede from their present rulers and establish a separate nation. Some, like the Irish IRA, the Spanish Basque group ETA, and the Armenian Secret Army for the Liberation of Armenia, use terrorist tactics. Dr. Jerrold M. Post, a psychiatrist who is an expert on terrorism, calls this type of terrorist the "nationalist-separatists." Croatia was one of the national groups lumped together after World War II to create the country now known as Yugoslavia. One of the terrorists described in Kellen's report was a Croat, Zvonko Busic, who grew up in a region where teaching Croatian history or language was forbidden. He became dedicated to the cause of Croatian independence and, in 1976, Busic, his wife, and three other Croatians hijacked a TWA airliner in New York with the intent of scattering thousands of political leaflets over New York, Montreal, and Croatia.

The other category of terrorists according to Dr. Post, are the "anarchist-ideologues," those who have rebelled against society in general and who advocate the violent overthrow of the present system.

Some experts have added a third category, international terrorism, which originates in the Middle East, and has state support and which involves the training of commandos. Some of these terrorists are like mercenaries, who hire out their services in other countries. Abu Nidal is said to be one such terrorist.

It is very difficult to assess the role that religion plays in terrorism, partly because Westerners have a limited understanding of the Muslim faith. Some experts, like Dr. Ariel Merari of Tel Aviv University, feel that the image of the suicidal religious fanatic has been exaggerated, and Israeli intelligence officers have confirmed his opinion in some cases. Interviews with suicidal terrorists captured alive reveal that some are blackmailed and others are tricked. A recent example of trickery involved an innocent Irish woman who was found to be carrying an explosive device in her suitcase, planted by her Arab boyfriend, who had told her he would meet her in Israel. The bomb would have blown her up along with the rest of the passengers on the El Al plane she was about to board. One writer and correspondent, Robin Wright, has stated that she was told by an influential Shi'ite leader, Sheikh Fadlallah, that suicide in the form of suicide missions is forbidden in his religion.

On the other hand, many experts believe that suicide missions are a new threat. According to one British expert with thirty years of experience in Cyprus, Malaya, and Palestine, the new terrorists are individuals who have been trained and prepared to be killed, and who want to die for their cause. The Ayatollah Khomeini of Iran and his Shi'ite followers are engaged in a holy war, and are actively training the young people of Iran to martyr themselves for the cause. In addition, Shi'ites from other countries go to Iran in order to learn the tactics of terrorism, so that the holy war can be carried out in other parts of the world, particularly in the West.

Despite their differences in backgrounds, personalities, and motivations, terrorists do have some characteristics in common. Most are young; the median age is 22.5 years. According to Dr. Charles Russell, formerly of the Air Force Office of Special Investigations, a typical terrorist is male, single, in his early twenties, from a middle- or upper-class family, university-educated, and joined a terrorist group while at school.

Many terrorists begin as dropouts who are bored and have no goals. A number have been university students, and some have been workers. They eventually discover that others, like themselves, feel alienated and disillusioned with society. When they find a group of peers who share the same feelings, many gain a sense of belonging for the first time in their lives. Complaints about injustice and inequality in society progress to the next stage of formulating plans of action to effect some change. Joining protest marches and demonstrating is the next step. Using more violent means such as rioting may then be followed by escalation to actual terrorism.

From the accounts of numerous terrorists, it is evident that they do not regard their violence as criminal, but are convinced that they are acting for the good of society. In addition, they consider their actions to be defensive in nature, that is, retaliation for wrongs perpetrated by society. Many start by violence against objects, not people—for instance, blowing up symbolic buildings or monuments. One expert calls terrorism a communication system, in which the message is expressed by violent actions. Often the stated intention is to force the authorities to retaliate with violence and further repression of the protesting group, thus gaining the support of the people.

Konrad Kellen has noted that two decisions are involved in becoming a terrorist: to break with society, and to join a terrorist group. He points out that there are many ways to break with society—for example, becoming a monk, a hermit, a criminal, a dropout. There are also many reasons, such as mental illness, religiosity, or laziness. Not everyone who rejects society becomes a terrorist.

Those who do become terrorists are often very frustrated with a system which cannot easily be changed, and they want the changes to occur immediately. Many are disgusted by the excessive materialism of modern society, and others are greatly affected by the injustices that they see. One terrorist joined a leftist group after seeing three policemen beat up an eighteen-year-old girl during a riot. He had been brought up to believe that the police always protect women and innocent people, but when he saw the strong oppress the weak, that instant became a turning point in his life.

Terrorists often tend to oversimplify issues, and their thinking is sometimes politically naive. They are self-righteous, dogmatic, and intolerant of deviations, even from their own followers. They are often convinced that their efforts, if they are successful, will result in a Utopian society.

Despite the high ideals expressed by many terrorists, such as the elimination of social injustice and oppression of minorities, terrorists paradoxically use violent methods to gain their objectives. They justify the means by the ends. They are able to kill because they see their victims not as people, but as objects and symbols of a system which needs to be destroyed.

Although experts have gathered much data about those who turn to terrorism, no one has really been able to identify with certainty what combination of personality characteristics, family constellations, and political and social influences produces a terrorist, or to predict who will take this path. The experts have not yet penetrated the mind of the terrorist.

SEVEN

Terrorists and Their Victims

EVERYONE is a potential victim of terrorism. A planeload of innocent vacationers may suddenly be seized at gunpoint, a business executive may be snatched from his car by terrorists who care nothing about the fate of their victim, but want only to further their cause. Such a situation of extreme stress can bring out strange, and unexpected, emotions and thoughts.

Experts in the field of terrorism have found that victims of human-induced violence react in remarkably similar ways, and follow a pattern which is characterized by several stages. The first stage is denial, shock, and disbelief. The person cannot believe that this is really happening to him or her.

In the second stage, with the dawning of reality, anxiety and fear arise. Contrary to popular opinion, most people who find themselves in terrifying situations do not react with desperate behavior, such as screaming, running, or jumping from windows. When someone is in a situation from which there is no escape, such as in a hostage situation, he is more likely to respond with a sort of paralysis, which Dr. Martin Symonds, a psychiatric consultant to the New York City Police Department, refers to as "frozen fright."

Civilian hostages generally do not protect themselves by attacking their captors, but they may do things like hiding or trying to slip away. A hostage may attempt to protect others who are weaker. One woman, held hostage in a bank robbery, threw herself on top of two children, shielding them with her body. She later reported, "I didn't think, I just responded, but I knew what I was doing." Most people seem to act automatically in this kind of situation, just as the woman in the bank did.

When a hostage is in a state of frozen fright, he feels powerless and isolated, and he may revert to immature ways of behaving, such as clinging and compliance. Sometimes the terror is disguised under a mask of calm friendliness. While some hostages are so frozen by fear that they can think of nothing but imminent death, others begin planning ways of escape.

Leon Richardson was an Australian businessman, visiting factories in Guatemala. Early one morning in February of 1981, as he was walking to his car, he found himself surrounded by eight men and women wearing camouflage fatigues and carrying automatic weapons. They poked a gun to his head and bundled him into a car, tying his hands and legs and blindfolding him. He was driven out into the countryside, and thrust into an underground cell, where he was to remain for more than three months.

The next three months proved to be a terrible ordeal. The

kidnappers took away Mr. Richardson's light after questioning him. He demanded that they return it, threw his food on the floor, and went on a hunger strike. Finally, after six days, the guards brought a bulb and a flashlight.

Mr. Richardson soon realized that this was to be a war of nerves, and that his captors were using psychological pressure on him to keep him submissive and cooperative. For instance, they acted friendly when he appeared depressed, and then at other times tried to upset him if his mood was good. He decided to counterattack by using the same techniques, deliberately keeping his emotional distance. This psychological contest was his way of fighting back and proving to himself that his kidnappers did not dominate him totally.

Believing that the worst enemy of a kidnap victim is morbid rumination, Mr. Richardson determined to fight for his survival by keeping up his hopes and by keeping himself active. He took note of every detail of his cell, listened to all the noises in the farmhouse above him, trying to determine the routines of his captors, and observed his guards carefully. He formulated escape plans, and actually made two attempts. Thinking about the possibility of escape helped him keep his sanity and self-respect.

He spent more than five hours a day doing exercises to keep himself physically fit, and he kept his mind occupied by writing technical reports, poetry, and even a cookbook. Above all, the fact that he never gave up hope helped him survive.

William F. Niehous, who spent more than three years as a hostage in the Venezuelan jungle, described his key to survival with the acronym FACES. F is for faith or hope; A stands for aspirations or goals; C, for communication; E, for exercising and eating; and S for sensitivity, or being human. Niehous, like Richardson and other survivors, did not allow himself to give up hope. He structured his time and kept himself occupied physically and mentally. He set goals for himself, telling himself he would live until some specific date, such as his wife's birthday, or Christmas. He made the ability to survive a source of self-esteem.

Establishing oneself as a human being in the eyes of one's captors may be an important factor for survival. Experts have found that when killing of hostages occurs, terrorists often kill those whom they consider dehumanized objects to be used. This was certainly the case during an incident that occurred in Holland in 1975, when South Moluccan terrorists took over a train and executed two of the hostages. On the second night, they selected Gerard Vaders as the third person to die. The terrorists gave him permission to relay a message to his family through another hostage, and they listened as Mr. Vaders explained his family situation and sent apologies to his wife for having failed in some ways. When he finished and told his captors that he was ready to die, they said, "No, someone else goes first." His life was spared because he was no longer an object or a symbol; he had become a human being.

Those hostages who are overly compliant and passive are more likely to be considered as objects than those who show resistance in small ways, just as Mr. Richardson did when he insisted on light for his cell and when he played psychological games with his captors.

Peter Hill was a passenger on TWA flight 847 which was

hijacked from Athens in June of 1985. He and other passengers were held hostage in Lebanon for fourteen days. Although fearful for his life, Mr. Hill responded in an active way by making escape plans, observing every detail around him, watching his captors, and even taking photographs secretly in an attempt to identify the place where they were being held. When two guards demanded that a hostage dance for them, Peter Hill told them firmly, "We don't dance for you or anybody!" The guards backed off. Peter Hill felt that it was important for the hostages to keep their dignity and self-respect, and he angrily lectured other hostages who showed friendliness or sympathy for the terrorists.

Just before the TWA hostages were released, they were driven through the streets, while television crews recorded the hostages and the crowds of people waving at each other. Peter Hill, however, raised his hand in an obscene gesture taught to him by some Israeli friends. He was hoping that the film would be shown on Jordanian television, which is also seen in Israel, and that the Israelis would recognize his gesture of defiance. This kind of defiant act, an attempt to mock the captors, is a common response among victims. Mr. Hill's reactions to being taken hostage were his way to "stand up and be counted." He said that he needed to prove something to himself about himself as a man.

Sir Geoffry Jackson, the British ambassador to Uruguay, was kidnapped by the Tupamaros, an ultra-leftist urban guerrilla terrorist group, and held hostage for 244 days. He remained so strong-minded and dignified that his guards were changed frequently in order to prevent him from convincing them that their cause was not justified.

The men described above kept themselves psychologically aloof from their captors in a variety of ways, but most people are probably not as disciplined or strong-willed. There is another, perhaps more common, phenomenon that occurs when hostages and hostage-takers remain in close contact with each other in a highly stressful situation. A strange, automatic, unconscious emotional bond often develops. It affects all ages and nationalities and both sexes, hostage-takers as well as victims, and is known as the Stockholm Syndrome, after the following incident.

In 1973, Jan-Erik Olsson, an escaped convict, walked into a Stockholm bank, took four young bank employees hostage, and held them prisoner in the bank vault for six days. Olsson demanded a large ransom, a car, and a plane to leave the country; he also persuaded them to release a fellow prisoner from jail and send him to the bank. During the course of the negotiations, one of the hostages spoke by telephone with the prime minister, telling him that they trusted the robbers, and were not afraid of them, but they were afraid that the police would do something to jeopardize their safety. At one point when Olsson allowed the police to enter in order to inspect, they found him with his arms around two of the women. Several times during the course of the siege, the robbers threatened the lives of the hostages, and when the police tried to break in by force, the gunmen shot and wounded an officer. When Olsson and his companion, who had joined him at the bank, finally surrendered, the hostages insisted on walking out of the vault with their captors, in order to prevent the police from gunning them down. The hostages and hostage-takers embraced and shook hands before the criminals were arrested and taken away.

Afterward, all the hostages insisted that they did not hate their captors, and that despite several instances of ill-treatment and threats, the robbers had been kind and considerate. They considered the police more of a threat than the criminals. They also felt sorry for the criminals, sympathizing with Olsson because of his unhappy past, his unjust treatment by the system, and his fear of returning to prison. When Olsson was interviewed, he said that he and his friend had been unable to kill the hostages, as they had originally intended, remarking that he had been "too soft."

There have been numerous instances of this kind of interaction between captors and captives. One airline attendant regularly visited the imprisoned terrorist who skyjacked her plane, and stated her intention of marrying him after his release. Some of the TWA passengers who were held hostage in Lebanon became very sympathetic to the terrorists, and one American businessman even offered to publicize and further their cause when he returned home. His feelings were quite different from those of his fellow passenger, Peter Hill, mentioned earlier.

Perhaps the most famous and widely publicized example of the Stockholm Syndrome was the case of Patty Hearst, the heiress who was abducted from her apartment by members of the Symbionese Liberation Army, a very small group of young radicals who were searching for a way to bring about revolutionary change. She was a frightened victim initially, but over a period of time, she began to form a bond with her kidnappers and started feeling sympathetic to their cause. She expressed her distrust of the police, and finally denounced her parents, her fiancé, and "the system." She became a full-fledged member of the SLA, changed her name to Tania, and participated in a bank robbery with the group. She even changed her style of speech, emulating her captors' expressions and scornful tone. Patty-Tania insisted that she had not been brainwashed or coerced, but that she had chosen to stay and fight.

The cases described are only a few examples of the phenomenon that Dr. Frederick J. Hacker has called the "poor-devil syndrome." Time and again, victims have said that they grew to understand their captors and to think of them as poor devils who deserved sympathy.

According to Dr. Frank Ochberg, Professor of Psychiatry at Michigan State University and a well-known expert on victims of terrorism, three conditions characterize the Stockholm Syndrome: the hostage experiences positive feelings toward the hostage-taker; he has negative feelings toward the police or other authorities responsible for rescue; and the hostage-taker reciprocates with positive feelings for the hostage.

The syndrome is an automatic response to the severe trauma of suddenly becoming a victim. Psychiatrists and psychologists who have studied this phenomenon theorize that terror induces a regression, or return to an infantile emotional state which is primitive and unconscious, and is related to the helplessness of infancy. The hostage is very much like an infant, since he is totally helpless and completely under the control of the captor. He is like a baby who is frightened of the outside world and depends on his parents to protect him and to meet his physical and emotional needs. Just as an infant places his trust in his all-powerful parents, the hostage feels trust and gratitude toward the all-powerful hostage-taker. In much the same way that abused children often cling to the very parent that abused them, a hostage may cling to the person who is threatening his life. The victim perceives the captor as good, because the captor is allowing him to live. This unconscious psychological mechanism helps the individual cope with an intolerable situation.

Interviews of many victims have revealed that those who experience this phenomenon are not aware of its true nature, and they express their emotions in terms that seem appropriate to them. In the case of Kristin, one of the Stockholm bank employees, her positive feelings were expressed as love for the young convict. In another situation, an older man compared his love for the young terrorists with the love of a father for his children.

The passage of time is a factor in the development of the Stockholm Syndrome. In one hijacking situation, when hostages were released in groups at intervals, the passengers who had spent more time with the hijackers appeared to have developed more positive feelings. In other incidents, the hostages' feelings did not seem to correlate with the amount of time spent with their captors. Other factors were operating. Some hostages slept for most of the time they were held; in this case, of course, there was minimal contact between the victims and hostage-takers, so no interaction took place. The interviewers speculated that the sleeping was a means of denial, a defense mechanism used by the victims to block out what was happening to them. Hostages who are physically abused react with very negative feelings, but even some people who suffer abuse may excuse the terrorists on the grounds that force was necessary, or that they themselves were to blame because they resisted. Researchers have found that if the victims are not abused, positive bonds are more likely to form between abductors and hostages. Another variable which influences the relationship is the presence of preexisting racial or ethnic hostility between captor and hostage. For instance, it has been noted that Israeli prisoners of Arab terrorists do not form positive bonds.

There is variation among hostages regarding the predisposition to relate to their captors. Some, like Patty Hearst, rapidly develop strong positive feelings. Others, like Peter Hill and Sir Geoffry Jackson, react in a very different manner. The situation of hostages may be compared with the situation of American prisoners of war in Korea who were subjected to brainwashing. It was found that those with strongly held beliefs and a definite philosophy of life did not succumb, while those who were more open-minded and unsure of themselves, and less experienced, were more likely to be indoctrinated.

Victims often feel that they are sharing a common experience with the hostage-takers, and may express hostility toward the police for keeping them trapped as well as the terrorists. Patty Hearst and Kristin, the Stockholm bank teller, were two among many other victims who demonstrated this reaction.

Many hostages experience an increase in fear when the incident appears to be approaching an end. They are afraid that something might go wrong during the rescue, and that they might be killed as well as the terrorists. This fear, coupled with distrust of the police, led one ex-hostage to remark, "I didn't know if they wanted to save me or get the criminals."

The last stage of the hostage's ordeal begins when he is rescued. Terrorism expert Brian Jenkins has noted that "It's not over when it's over." Most ex-hostages feel that no one else can possibly understand what they have been through. They may experience guilt and depression about their behavior during captivity, blaming themselves for not having acted in a more heroic manner, or for sympathizing too much with their captors. Many feel that perhaps in some way they were responsible for their plight, a feeling which may unfortunately be shared by others. There is a common myth that if bad things happen to people, they must be deserved. According to Jenkins, it is their own fear that makes it difficult for people to accept the fact that the same thing could happen to them; therefore they conclude that the victim must be different and that he must have done something to cause his own misfortune.

Dr. Frank Ochberg has estimated that between one-third and one-half of the former hostages he has interviewed have suffered psychological symptoms. Problems include depression, insomnia, nightmares, anxiety attacks, phobias, obsessions, and feelings of alienation. Of the survivors of the Moluccan train hijacking, one-third developed train phobias. Some victims experience continued replay, or flashbacks, of the traumatic events. They may feel jumpy for weeks or months, and they may have difficulty in concentrating. Some former hostages have difficulty dealing with their angry, vengeful feelings, and remain on guard against the rest of the world. Both former hostages and families may have reentry problems, and family relationships may suffer.

Victims have a great need to be allowed to express feelings and emotions. Families, friends, and therapists can serve by allowing them to tell and retell their story. This process aids the victim to integrate and resolve his experience. Released hostages are often angry because others have been negotiating for their lives and they need help in regaining their sense of self-esteem and power.

Being taken hostage can have positive effects. Some survivors undergo profound changes in attitude—for example, experiencing a deeper faith, or cementing a relationship between husband and wife. Many ex-hostages have gained a greater appreciation of life. They have become less attached to material things, and more tolerant and generous with others.

EIGHT

Target: Americans Overseas

An American business executive arrives at the Rome airport behind schedule for the flight that will take her to an important meeting in Paris. She rushes to the ticket counter, then to the boarding area, but the hurried approach to her flight is halted. The airport bristles with state-of-the-art anti-terrorist technology. There are increased security checks, and her attache case not only passes through X-ray equipment but it is thoroughly checked for a false bottom or lid. The executive is slightly irritated, but she knows she should be glad that the security is tight. A bomb that was smuggled on the plane in any attache case could eliminate her business in France or even eliminate her and the other passengers on the plane.

Although recent terrorist attacks have increased fears in travelers, American executives have been targets for a long time. Many terrorists are leftists who oppose capitalism; they destroy people and buildings representing a system they abhor, they kidnap individuals to get money and publicity for their causes. Multinational firms are leaning toward a low profile in foreign countries and many Americans who travel are trying not to look like Americans. American Telephone & Telegraph Company has issued a booklet for employees who travel abroad on how to cope with terrorism.

Since protection for government and military personnel has improved recently, the corporate community considers itself to be a prime target. Security for company employees is not new.

In 1850 Allan Pinkerton founded an agency to protect trains from robberies. In 1909 William Burns formed the International Detective Agency as a private protection force for businesses. These companies provide bodyguards for individuals or watchmen and electronic surveillance for plants and office buildings. Risks International provides computer-updated information on terrorism such as kidnappings, hijackings, bombings, and attacks against facilities around the world, as well as a consulting service aimed at protecting businesses and their employees. Antone Security, Inc. offers expert advice in many fields, including threat analysis and driving to avoid terrorists. There are companies which armor-plate autos. Some companies specialize in negotiating the release of kidnapped individuals, cutting back the ransom and returning the hostages alive. As more terrorist actions occur, more businesses are formed to deal with the problems. Over the past ten years, the security business has been one of the world's fastest-growing industries.

Terrorists find it efficient to get money from businesses either by ransom, which is paid to free a kidnapped executive, or by extortion, which is paid on the threat of kidnapping or plant destruction. Businesses know their personnel have been well trained and are valuable to the company, so they are willing to pay large sums to retrieve kidnap victims. Terrorists know this too.

Most companies doing business internationally have insurance which covers ransom, a crisis management team which decides in general terms how the company will respond to a threat or deed, and have access to a negotiator who will deal with the terrorists regarding their demands. The crisis manager is part of the company and has the job of deciding ahead of any trouble just what the company will do in the way of publicity and settlement. All the vulnerable employees have been part of that decision making. The negotiator is an outsider who will deal with the terrorists at the time of trouble. Both parts of the team are necessary. Using a negotiator serves several ends: a specially trained third party involves the terrorists for extra time which can often be used to find the hiding place of the victim and increase the chances of hostage survival. And an independent negotiator is essential when treating with mid-Eastern terrorists as they consider direct dealing demeaning.

When terrorists kidnap an executive, it is usually someone they have studied very carefully. As a rule, they want to maintain a low profile. They have large amounts of spare time and little to fill it, so they read newspapers with great avidity, learning all they can about the executive individually, and about the company in general. When the hideout of a terrorist group was examined recently, a card file and carefully catalogued newspaper clippings were found, all relating to one firm and two of its top men. Everything was noted about those men—where they usually ate lunch, with whom, what foods. Did they use the elevators in their buildings or the stairs? Did they play tennis? With whom? Where? Did they like opera? Soccer? Baseball? Dancing? What sort of transportation and what route did they follow to and from work? Any sort of information is useful to a would-be kidnapper.

Surprise and knowledge are both on the side of the terrorist. Most kidnappings take place when the victim is in an automobile, quite close to home and either on the way to or from work. Everyone tends to relax in a car and however varied the route can be in the middle of the trip, it is hard to find more than one or two ways to go at the ends. The kidnapper has thorough knowledge of the type and color of the car, what security arrangements have been made, who drives and what sort of events confuse the driver. When Hans-Martin Schleyer of Daimler-Benz was going home from work one night, the intersection nearest his home was blocked by a yellow Mercedes and a woman pushing a baby carriage across the street. The driver, though trained in defensive techniques, instinctively veered to avoid hitting either impediment and struck the curb, whereupon he and the police in the security car behind were all shot and Schleyer was abducted by members of the Baader-Meinhof Gang. The demand of the terrorists was the release of eleven political prisoners. The German government decided not to satisfy the gang's desire for publicity and released no information to the media while their negotiator worked. Negotiations went on for some six weeks but were unsuccessful. Schleyer was murdered.

While costs to the perpetrators are few, it is expensive for a business to be the target of terrorist actions. Businesses must finance increased security, training in self-protection, insurance for ransoms, costs of negotiator fees, loss of employee time, and diminished production. Morale in a company declines, tensions are high, and insecurity is rife. All these lead to production lessened in quality and quantity.

American embassies, which certainly represent capitalism, are the focus of much terrorism. The State Department pays extra money as a danger allowance to Americans posted to such hazardous areas as Lebanon, Afghanistan, Uganda, El Salvador, Colombia, and Kuwait.

At the Kuwait embassy all employees have been trained in physical self-defense and emotional self-protection by mobile training teams hired by the United States government. The ambassador has also learned to assemble and fire several different weapons. There are unannounced drills, similar to fire drills in American schools. During these the Marines on guard spring to action with rifles at the ready and the rest of the staff heads for assigned rooms, stocked as bomb shelters, to wait out the emergency. The embassy building is protected by razor wire and tank traps, but most of the staff live elsewhere, so they are trained in home security such as alarms and guard dogs, and learn where to look for the probable car bomb (usually in the wheel wells or the exhaust pipe).

Families living in troubled areas of the world have special problems. Even very young children have to be taught to vary routines and activities, to give out no information about the family, to avoid places where there is danger. American children living in Rome cannot be allowed to go to fast food restaurants for fear of bombs. Schools for American children in Rome are guarded by armed police, as are the school buses on which the children ride, and the schools take an active role in training the children to protect themselves. In many countries, children are taught to dress as do the children of the host country, to use public transportation or inconspicuous private cars, to check under theatre seats for suspicious parcels, and not to pick up anything seen lying about, as it may well be a bomb.

American tourists have become prime targets of terrorists. Terrorism thrives on a climate of fear, and terrorists abroad succeeded in causing the "panic of the summer of '86," a time when travel bureaus were besieged with requests to change reservations from trouble spots to vacations in safer areas.

Ninety-five percent of the reservations Americans held in Egypt for the next two years were cancelled. Group tours were cancelled in large numbers, so advance bookings for all of Europe were down 20 to 30 percent, and those to southern Europe declined even more.

Very few tourists attended the usually crowded Easter service in Jerusalem in 1986. The Abu Nidal group proudly claimed the shooting of a British tourist later in the spring.

Despite pleas by the Pope for greater protection of tourists, many would-be visitors cancelled reservations for Rome after that airport was involved in several hijackings and was the scene of a massacre by a Palestinian group.

Libyan-claimed bombings in Paris and reported lax security at the Athens airport made travelers wary of France and Greece.

Since terrorism is used to shock and stress a group far larger than the one which is actually attacked, it is not surprising that recent actions against Americans have done just that. By early 1986 Americans became aware that areas of the world where we represent capitalism to Marxists, or areas where we represent heretics to faithful Muslims are particular danger spots. The "fertile crescent" of terrorism is the Mideast, but Latin America and Europe have been called the "playground of terrorism." Terrorists will go to great lengths to carry out their plans and anyplace in the world is a possible site of trouble.

Many tourists changed their plans and headed for American cities and national parks. Others decided on Scandinavia, New Zealand, or Eastern-bloc countries such as Yugoslavia and the USSR where there is little terrorism. Overseas travelers avoided group tours and American airlines as too visible, and most used smaller airports than they formerly did.

Even though it has been pointed out that more Americans die in their bathtubs than are killed by terrorists, and though Gary Sick, a foreign affairs expert with the Ford Foundation, pointed out that more Americans were killed by lightning each year than by terrorists, many people changed vacation plans. There is little or no media coverage of deaths in bathtubs or by lightning bolts. Death by terrorism is big news.

Not all travelers are tourists. Many American businesses have plants and offices abroad which are staffed by American executives and visited often by representatives from the home office. European companies have American offices. Governments have military and civilian employees stationed in other countries. Children fly unescorted to visit families. School groups travel to learn how the rest of the world lives. There are huge numbers of people flying back and forth across oceans and continents.

Since surprise is one weapon that is very hard to combat, it is usually on the side of the terrorists, but airports are revising their security plans and airlines are acting to forestall terrorism in many ways. Searches of baggage and passengers are far more thorough now than even one year ago. Service people such as cleaners and caterers are being checked more carefully on employment and watched more carefully as they work. Passengers are being taken to the airport in airline transportation rather than in private cars. At some airports everyone—workers, passengers, and any other person who enters—are being subjected to at least X-ray search. High fences are being built around some airports. Dogs, and even gerbils, trained to sniff out explosives, are being used.

Israel and its state-owned airline El Al, have implemented some of these and even stronger security measures with great success. Officials pass baggage through a low-pressure chamber to trip pressure-sensitive detonators on the ground before they have a chance to explode in the air. The discovery by El Al employees of some 20 kilos of explosives in the handbag of a woman who had already passed through general airport security at London's Heathrow airport, and who had already been body-searched by the airline is an example of the value of thoroughness. Her handbag was searched one last time as she boarded the plane and the explosives, light and easily hidden, were found. It is thought that the woman had no idea these were in her baggage and that they were planted by her boyfriend. She and the entire plane were scheduled to explode twenty minutes off the ground.

Here are some other examples of increased security procedures:

Iraqi Airlines has banned all hand baggage, even newspapers. Its passengers are searched once upon entering the airport and again as they approach the plane to board.

Alia, the Jordanian airline, X-rays hand baggage at both check-in and boarding, in addition to searching boarding passengers.

Swiss Air hand-searches all carry-on materials and body-searches all passengers.

Pan Am has announced ALERT, an in-house-supported security system which will increase security in every airport they use with a new, highly sophisticated screening system.

Despite advances, it is hard for airlines to keep up with terrorists. Guns can be made of plastic so that only springs of metal show under X-ray. The Austrian-made Glock 17 is a pistol made almost entirely of plastic, is easy to take apart, and the resulting small parts can be hidden in baggage which passes airport scanners. Then the gun can quickly be reassembled in the washroom of the airport or plane. Explosive materials known as plastiques and hexogen are not spotted by X-ray, and can be shaped to resemble any object at all to avoid suspicion.

A new detector has been developed by a Cambridge, Massachusetts, firm, American Science and Engineering, which can spot plastic weapons. Common X-ray machines spot metal that is heavy enough to absorb most of the X-rays, but plastics and other low-density materials are not seen. The new system creates two sets of images on two screens; one shows objects that absorb X-rays and the other shows objects that scatter them. The system uses a pencil-thin ray that scans the whole object point by point, rather than through the wide beams of X-ray which a suitcase usually moves through on a conveyer belt. Scanned in this way, the pattern of deflected beams provides a precise image. There are also devices which detect plastics by their nitrogen content.

A system developed by a Canadian firm, Sciex, detects contraband cargo by sensing vapors which are then analysed to reveal drugs and explosives. Used in combination with a British-made zoom lens, which will scan and record crate contents, this will be an effective deterrent. But even these detectors are not 100 percent effective.

Airline executives are reexamining current safety measures and adding others to ensure that their security people stay alert. In some cases, employees watching scanners are relieved every twenty minutes to guard against boredom. Flights are cancelled to avoid trouble spots. TWA rerouted its flights to Cairo through Paris and Frankfurt after troubles in 1986 made Athens and Rome unpopular spots with pilots and travelers.

The problems of security in the Arab world are complicated by perfectly innocent Arab workers who travel about the mid-East by plane carrying their goods in parcels which are oddly shaped and so wrapped that they could, and do, contain anything from a television set to food for dinner. The same travelers speak in many dialects, which makes it difficult for airport personnel to screen them at all.

In view of the interest both airlines and governments have

in travelers, it seems likely that measures will be implemented everywhere, especially in the mid-East where security has been lax and religious fanaticism is rife.

Terrorism aims to disrupt the normal flow of life for the targeted group. Terrorism also aims to publicize the activists. Both of these ends have been achieved. In 1986, shortly after a bomb ripped a jagged hole in the side of a TWA plane as it descended toward Athens and four Americans were sucked to their deaths, a phone call, received by a Beirut news agency, claimed that the bomb had been planted by a group called the Arab Revolutionary Cells and was "in retaliation for American arrogance." That group was hitherto unknown to authorities and while it may have been responsible, the act could have been planned months before by someone else who just didn't get the credit. After some acts of terrorism there are many groups that claim them. They all try to put their cause before the public in any way possible.

NINE

Terrorism and the Media

TERRORISTS have invited the press for interviews with their hostages. The television network has questioned whether or not this might be inflating the terrorists to the position of folk heroes; on the other hand, the networks may be increasing public revulsion against terrorist acts. They decide to go ahead with the interview. It may further the terrorist cause, but it *is* news.

More than a hundred journalists shout at each other and elbow for space to get near the hostages. Cameramen climb on tabletops to get better angles for their pictures. The men who are guarding the hostages erect a barrier of chairs in front of them, then remove the hostages from the room because of some scuffles between the journalists and security men. The press conference brings no news other than the assurance that the hostages are still alive.

The questions are often asked, "Do the media help or hinder in hostage situations? What is the responsibility of the press in covering terrorism? How can the media report terrorism without magnifying its effect?" Car bombs detonated on city streets, airplanes exploding in midair, innocent people killed in railroad stations and airport terminals are newsworthy. As terrorist incidents increase, questions about media coverage increase. There is controversy about whether or not news media are providing news that helps the public to understand the central issues of the day or acting as a megaphone for the terrorists. The problem is complex and there is no simple answer.

In November of 1986, the media reported secret involvement of the United States in arms shipments to Iran in efforts to win the release of American hostages. While some people blamed the media for reporting covert actions, others praised them for bringing the public's attention to what might have been an attempt to get around American law. The United States policy of not giving in to terrorism was brought into question.

News of terrorism seems to be everywhere. Many Americans think of terrorism as something that has just been happening in the last few decades. Perhaps this is because more Americans were killed and wounded by terrorists in a period of 30 months than in the previous 13 years. It is also due to the fact that more Americans are exposed to media coverage than ever before.

The media play an important role in many kinds of terrorism, for terrorists know that the world is their captive audience. Television brings the viewer to the scene in such a way that he or she is the participant in a dangerous act while in a safe place. The bloody horror of a terrorist act has a certain amount of entertainment value even while those who watch are shuddering in protest and find the action repulsive. The amount of violence on television shows attests to its appeal. While the media tend to focus on the violence of a terrorist act and obscure the issue behind the confrontation, researchers are working toward guidelines for the media to make more certain that they are part of the solution rather than part of the problem.

Many experts have said that the terrorist needs the media as a fish needs water. Terrorists know that the media will spread the effect of their deeds; their ultimate target is not the immediate victim but the national or global audience of the media. Whether or not the public remains in sympathy with the victim is controlled, to some degree, by the way the incident is presented and by the remarks made by news analysts. At best, the role of the media is to balance the right of access to newsworthy events, to gather and publish it freely against potential injury of hostages and loss of life.

In some cases, television viewers have shared the ordeal of a kidnapped victim, and the media have helped to bring about a safe return. But there have been incidents in which reporters have interfered with hostage negotiations in their clamor for news. Obviously, a reporter is looking for the best story possible, and hostage events are dramatic, often violent life-and-death situations. The families of hostages who are anxiously waiting for the outcome provide a human interest element. The give-and-take of the negotiations makes good copy.

Lack of responsible judgment on the part of some reporters has been cited in a number of cases. Picture a situation in which the negotiators are using a hidden mirror to see what is happening inside a building. The terrorists are glued to their television set when the information about the mirror is revealed by an announcer who is reporting news to the public and, of course, to them. The terrorists immediately cover the mirror, and an important element of safety is lost. In another actual case, reporters telephoned people who lived near the scene of a terrorist incident asking what they could see. Their responses revealed the approach of a team of men who were trying to arrive on the scene without the knowledge of the terrorists. Such incidents have helped to create the gulf that exists between some law enforcement agents and the media.

Certainly the media supply the terrorist with an audience far greater than they could hope to reach without modern communications. It increases the climate of fear, an important motive for terrorist acts. The killing of innocent people, the kidnappings, the hostage-takings all make news that terrorists use to further their causes.

Perhaps the most famous case of the use of the media by terrorists is the oft-quoted event in which terrorists took control of the television screens. On February 27, 1975, German terrorists kidnapped Peter Lorenz, a lawyer and chairman of the West Berlin branch of Germany's conservative Christian Democratic Union. While Lorenz, a mayoral candidate, was held in a room beneath a furniture store that had been prepared as a cell, members of the West German Baader-Meinhof Gang of terrorists demanded the release of six of their comrades from prison. Melvin Lasky, a TV editor, told of his experiences in *Encounter* magazine:[1]

"For 72 hours, we just lost control of the medium, it was theirs, not ours . . . We shifted shows to meet their timetable. Our cameras had to be in position to record each of the released prisoners as they boarded the plane to freedom, and our news coverage had to include prepared statements at their dictate . . . It's never happened before. There is plenty of underworld crime on our screens but up to now Kojak and Columbo were always in charge. . . . Now it was the real thing, and it was the gangsters who wrote the script and programmed the mass media. We preferred to think that we were being 'flexible,' but actually we were just helpless. . . ."

Although many terrorists receive wide media coverage, others remain faceless individuals who live far away and who are a threat only to a relatively few individuals for whom most people have little concern. The announcement of a kidnapping of an American businessman may no longer make headlines on the front page. Buried among other news is an item about a man who was abducted as he stepped into the back seat of his car. He has been whisked away from the scene by a driver who has replaced his regular chauffeur. Accounts of the incident include little detailed background of the victim.

Later it is discovered that the victim is a well-known champion of peace, a well-loved citizen, and a person whose disappearance is a concern of the entire country. With the next account there is a formal photograph of the man in the

[1] Melvin J. Lasky, "Ulrike Meinhof and the Baader-Meinhof Gang." *Encounter*, vol. 44, June, 1975, pp 15–16.

newspapers. The incident is mentioned on the television news. The search for the terrorists begins, and reports of possible witnesses of the men and women responsible for the kidnapping are well publicized. Police and other security groups are at work, and hopes are high that the man will be rescued.

Within a few days of the kidnapping, the terrorists provide a photograph of the man as he stands in front of some of the posters that illustrate their slogans. At the same time, the demands for his release are made known. He will be freed in exchange for a large number of fellow terrorists who are now in prison. The alternative is torture of their captive. If their demands are not met within three days, they will kill him.

The media play a major and a critical role in the hostage negotiations, but do not interfere with the role of the negotiators. The citizens of his country are horrified, and decisions must be made. Will the man be returned, traumatized but physically unharmed? Will the next picture of him be one of a body in the trunk of a car or in a coffin? Will he be able to escape? Will the demands of the terrorists be met? Should they be?

Some individuals blame the media for inciting further terrorism just by their coverage of it. The great exposure of the horrors of war through the media has made that type of conflict increasingly unattractive in the world, not only to Americans, but for a number of nations, according to Brian Jenkins, an expert on terrorism, in his testimony before the Senate in 1985. He stated that we look forward to an era of warfare in the future that is quite different from the warfare that we saw in the first half of this century.

Mr. Jenkins continued his testimony as follows, "We look forward to an era of warfare in which at times limited conventional combat will be replaced by, or accompanied by, guerrilla war, as well as by international terrorism, or a mix of these things. . . . It is very difficult to get people to understand the issues at stake, what are the strategies and tactics being pursued and how can we effectively combat them."

The hostage crisis during which Iran held Americans hostage for 444 days, from November 4, 1979, to January 20, 1981, was so important that American media held a nightly hostage "show" which is considered to have led to ABC's "Nightline." Sam Lipski states in *The Bulletin,* an Australian newsmagazine, that the Lebanese Shi'ites developed this art form to a new level. He suggests that silencing, or at least muffling, the global megaphone of the terrorists would not end international terrorism, but it would help to weaken it.

The role of television in reporting the acts of terrorists is a difficult one. Ray S. Cline, another expert in the field, testified before the same Senate hearings of the Ninety-ninth Congress (1985) that the hostile states that sponsor terrorism are very clear that terrorism is a bit of street theater. He said, "It is a form of dramatic presentation of ideas, and the target is the American public. That is why television is such a beautiful instrument for them. If our television acts innocently and descriptively, they give the terrorists a magnificent chance to sell their message, which is they will win and it is foolish to resist, that Americans are not smart enough to, nor determined enough to, resist this kind of attack."

The wise use of the media is discussed by Richard Clutterbuck, an authority on terrorism, in his book *Guerrillas and*

Terrorists. He quotes an old Chinese proverb, "Kill one, frighten ten thousand," and notes that the strongest single factor which leads governments to give way to terrorists, internationally or internally, is television. In addition to magnifying the actions of terrorists, it brings their violence on a personal level into the home of every citizen in the land in which they are operating as well as to people in many other countries.

How can the media help in the solution of the problem of terrorism? Their sole role is to transmit information, and no one believes that they can erase terrorism. The press and television reporters have no choice about covering terrorist acts, for terrorism is newsworthy. Everyone is a potential victim, the actions deviate from the norm, they have considerable value as adventure and entertainment, and the actions affect a large segment of the population. Few would suggest that there is any value in restraining the free press and so deny the citizens of a democracy the right to know what is happening. But there is a difference between the public's right to know and the right to know everything. The right to a story is not as important as a victim's right to life. It has been suggested that the media could use some restraint in covering the actions of terrorists.

The value of restraint is illustrated by Clutterbuck at the end of his book through the story told to him by a fireman who observed a torso from which all clothing had been blown away, arms and legs were severed, and the head was just a spongy mass. No reporters were permitted near the scene. The fireman wanted to call in television crews to send the horror to the homes of the public in the hope that this would let them see how awful terrorism really is. But a few days later, he changed his mind about this. He was called to extinguish a fire that was set in the home of a man who had painted an emblem on the wall. This emblem caused the indignation of his neighbors and initiated the fire setting. Suppose they had seen the horror of the torso. Many more homes might have been set on fire, and the backlash might have been uncontrollable.

Lt. Col. Harold Wilbur of the United States Marine Corps supports the idea of a blue-ribbon panel to be created to study self-regulation of the media in terrorist situations. This could develop a working rapport among the key "players" in a terrorist incident such as law enforcement, legal, and security representatives, hostage negotiators, and members of the media. Possible media participation with authorities in simulated terrorist incidents could prove to be an invaluable training aid for all involved.

In Ireland, the appearance of terrorism on television is considered an incitement to murder. Incidents are believed to inspire other terrorists and potential terrorists. The general public is already aware of the view of the terrorists, so interviews with them are not considered newsworthy.

In England, a ten-year agreement between the British press and Scotland Yard has kept kidnapping out of the news until the cases have been resolved and this seems to have helped lower the rate of kidnapping. However, this approach can backfire. When the British Broadcasting System showed the picture of a girl who had been kidnapped on television, a woman called to say that she could have helped earlier if she had known about the kidnapping. She had seen this girl playing near a neighborhood house.

On May 5, 1986, Abul Abbas was interviewed on NBC news for two minutes. He is the convicted mastermind behind the seajacking of the *Achille Lauro* in October of 1985 and many other terrorist acts. This caused considerable controversy. Ambassador Robert Oakley, head of the State Department's counterterrorism office, accused NBC of being an accomplice to terrorism by giving publicity to Abbas. Others suggested that the interview might encourage terrorism. NBC defended its action as the right of a free press and the right of the American people to know about terrorism and the dangers of the world in which we live. According to Abbas, his 1,200-strong Palestine Liberation Front now plans to bring terrorism to the United States, and President Reagan has now become enemy number one. The United States government apparently did not know that Abbas was on a secret visit to Algeria at the time of the interview. He left the country for an unknown destination before he could be captured.

The coverage of terrorist events, with restraint, appears to be the most acceptable answer. Daniel Schorr, a senior correspondent for CBS, remarked at the Conference on International Terrorism in 1984 conducted by the Jonathan Institute, a private research foundation, that people in the news business should impose some voluntary limits because if they don't "there may come a time when they are imposed on us."

Certainly, the media can play a major role in developing public awareness of the real aims of terrorists and of how terrorism can be prevented. Better cooperation between the media and law enforcement representatives is an important goal for the future. The role of the media is an important consideration in counterterrorist planning.

TEN

Searching for Answers

WHO? When? Where will the terrorists strike next?

Will the mastermind of a terrorist organization sit in front of a computer and orchestrate an attack with a nuclear weapon? Will terrorism with high tech weapons escalate to more spectacular and more destructive acts? No one knows the answers to these questions. Nor is there any easy or single answer to the problem of how to counteract or prevent terrorism.

Many uninformed individuals talk about reasons for terrorism and make suggestions for easy solutions. Let's look at some examples, using fictitious names for real people.

Maud said that terrorism will stop if we detach ourselves from the Arab world. She says all Arabs are shifty, impossible people. Maud never knew any Arabs in the United States, and she was sure she would not like them if she did. But she needed some very special dental work and the only dentist

who could help her was an Arab who had come to this country several years ago. After a few visits to the dentist, Maud
no longer made blanket statements about Arabs. She liked
her dentist both for his skill and his personality, and she also
gave some thought to the fact that much of the oil she used
to heat her house came from Arab countries. Maud decided
she needed to do some thinking about her decision making
and her tendency to generalize. Since some Arabs are among
the principal targets of Libyan-supported terrorism, any
statement that accuses all Arabs of terrorism is obviously false.

Bob said the Jews were the cause of all terrorist problems.
He complained about the turmoil in the Middle East, and he
often told the story about a Palestinian friend who had to
leave his home when Israel became a nation. "No wonder the
Palestinians are mad," he often remarked. "If I were chased
from my homeland, I would blow up Jews, too." Certainly,
much of modern terrorism is tied to the Arab-Israeli conflict,
but many people are striving for better ways of dealing with
the problem. Recent surveys show that 50 percent of Jews
feel that Palestinians have a right to a homeland on the West
Bank and Gaza as long as it does not threaten Israel. Another
25 percent were undecided, and only a quarter disagreed.
Even if the Arab-Israeli problem were solved, terrorism would
continue on many other fronts.

Linda has much the same feelings as Bob about the rights
of people who are downtrodden. All terrorists have grievances, according to Linda, and they are driven to horrible acts
by their passions. She believes that terrorists indulge in kidnapping, murder, arson, and other horrible acts because they
are unable to achieve their goals by other means. She feels

that such people are beyond the bounds of ordinary morals, so that when they kill innocent people they should not really be considered murderers. Scholars note that many people who have lost their homelands and have other grievances do not automatically turn to terrorism.

Pat sends money to his cousins in Ireland to help them fight the "British murderers." One of his cousins was killed when he was placing a bomb in the car of a Protestant leader. "If the Irish Catholics were not mistreated," Pat says, "my cousin would be alive today." Like Linda, he supports the theory of grievances.

Many people adhere to the theory of grievances as applied to terrorism, but experts on the subject disagree with its validity. A grievance is never an excuse for killing innocent people, but there appears to be a reason for the wide acceptance of this theory. According to Midge Decter, Executive Director of the Committee for the Free World, and a contributor to *Terrorism: How the West Can Win,* terrorism is organized political warfare, not a response to social conditions. She suggests the following comparison. If we believe that terrorists are suffering from a social disease that they carry in somewhat the same way innocent animals carry rabies, we no longer have to make a decision about them. Since we then feel that they have no normal human responsibilities because they are suffering, we consider their acts to be general misfortune, somewhat like a mine disaster. So, if we deny a person the moral responsibility for the consequences of terrorist acts, we no longer have to feel any burden of moral responsibility for their actions. For example, if a man who belongs to a group that wants to help the poor beats up a rich man so he can further his cause, we might say he is really acting in a way that he believes will help society. Can we close our eyes to the fate of the rich man? In the same sense, if a terrorist who believes he needs to kill in order to bring about a change in society blows up a busload of children to promote his cause, should we just consider his grievance? Doing so could make it easier to be morally lazy.

Many experts agree that the terrorism problem cannot be solved by establishing a peace treaty in the Middle East, isolating nations such as Iran, or eliminating missile batteries in Libya. Policy makers in the United States and other countries have spent a greal deal of time in the last fifteen years trying to improve antiterrorism policies. Some experts have concluded that an expanded menu of tools and tactics for use in each situation may be better than any single declared policy. Certainly, many policies and programs are being expanded at the present time. A vast amount of literature has been produced on ways to combat terrorism, but much of it is vague and ideological.

While much policy making remains covert, there are serious reports available for those who wish to delve further into the subject. One report of a panel on terrorism is "Combating Terrorism: A Matter of Leverage," published by the Center for Strategic and International Studies, Georgetown University, Washington, D.C. in June of 1986. Robert Kupperman, chairman of this panel of thirty private and government experts, notes that much work remains to be done in our efforts to combat terrorism. For example, he states that "The potential for attacks against the technological infrastructure of the United States or chemical and biological attacks has been inadequately explored." Complex service networks such as electric power grids, thousands of miles of oil and gas pipelines, huge communication webs in the business and financial worlds, water supplies that come from long distance . . . these and more are vulnerable. Dr. Kupperman suggests that articulate citizen concern could prompt awareness that might lead to sensible precautionary measures for large-scale emergencies that could upset our daily living.

This is just one of the ways that the public can help to prevent and combat terrorism. Other ways range from simple everyday activities to learning more about what can and what cannot be done to combat terrorism and advocating responsible action in areas in addition to the above.

Increased public awareness of passengers on planes and trains is one of the simpler measures that can be developed to prevent terrorism. Suspicious objects and abandoned packages on overhead racks in buses and planes or under the seats that have been reported by individuals have frequently turned out to be explosives.

Improvement of security measures at airports is continuing, but there is general agreement that it is impossible to develop completely foolproof protection. Travelers have been commended for their cooperation during delays caused by increased security checks. As much of the panic among travelers, described in an earlier chapter, subsides, the military forces continue to increase training in antiterrorism. Fast-acting commando units have played an important role in preventing terrorist incidents. Ambassador Robert Oakley, head of the U.S. State Department's counterterrorism activities, reports that more than 120 terrorist attacks against U.S. citizens were aborted in the year 1985.

Retaliation against terrorists by police measures and military action is a subject of much controversy. The raid at Entebbe in Uganda by Israeli troops is often cited as an example of the defeat of terrorists by fighting back. On June 27, 1976, shortly after passengers of Air France flight 139 en route from Tel Aviv to Paris took off from Athens, they heard the voice of a female terrorist announce that the plane had been hijacked by a unit of the Popular Front for the Liberation of Palestine. The voice was that of Gabrielle Kroecher-Teidemann, a friend of Carlos and one of the kidnappers of the OPEC oil ministers in Vienna. Other terrorists on the plane soon produced weapons, and passengers underwent intimate body searches. The crew was forced to fly to Libya for refueling, and at this point a woman who was pregnant and hemorrhaging was released. The rest of the hostages were flown to Entebbe airport in Uganda.

In Uganda, native soldiers were waiting for the plane and they quickly surrounded it. A new group of terrorists under the leadership of Antonio Bouvier, a man who shared safe houses with Carlos in London, herded the 256 passengers into an abandoned terminal lounge. Sticks of dynamite were scattered among them. After an appearance by Idi Amin, who was rabidly anti-Israeli, the Jewish passengers were separated from the others. During negotiations for the release of 53 of their "freedom fighters" held in Israel, the terrorists released all but 106 people. While the negotiations were taking place, the Israelis were secretly preparing to fly two thousand miles from Israel to Uganda, land there and overpower the terrorists and the soldiers of Uganda, and fly back with the hostages. The rescue was carried out in only fifty minutes between landing and takeoff. Only the loss of the Israeli leader, Jonathan Netanyahu, three hostages, and a seventy-three-year-old hospitalized woman, Dora Bloch, believed to have been murdered by orders of Idi Amin, marred the success of this bold and daring mission. The terrorists, all members of the Carlos gang, were not center stage in this action. The spotlight belonged to the victims and those who rescued them.

Fighting back rather than giving in is a policy that has worked well in some cases, but it is not always so. The United States raid on Libya is still a matter of controversy, with some people pointing out that the action appeared to solidify Arabs, even though many of them had not been supportive of Qaddafi. Many people consider the raid a form of First World terrorism, and debate the "surgical strike" which killed many innocent people while the administration claims that they were casualties of a necessary action. Still others point out that the number of terrorist acts immediately following the raid were not as numerous as expected, and cite the apparent efforts of Syria to cooperate in the reduction of terrorism immediately after the raid. Ultimately, European countries reduced the number of Libyan diplomats, pledged better cooperation on intelligence activities, agreed to share information and extradite suspects. Many experts feel that Europe's opposition to military action but willingness to cooperate in other ways was a more mature approach to countering terrorism than the use of military force.

One of the steps in preventing terrorism on which almost

everyone agrees is the effort to improve negotiation techniques and putting them into action quickly. Many negotiation teams are being trained to secure the safe release of victims. Experts point out that the selection of negotiators is, in itself, an important step, and that the less said in public the better. That messages should be blunt and simple is another recommendation. A number of security companies have trained consultants who are available to help negotiating teams deal with kidnappings and other forms of terrorism. Certainly, negotiations are too important to be left to amateurs.

Intelligence has been called the first line of defense against terrorism. By keeping careful records on all known terrorists, by learning everything possible about terrorist organizations, motives, and ideology, many actions have been prevented. In West Germany, a computer called the "Kommisar" stores information such as names, code names, safe houses, disguises, false passport use, appearances, contacts, and as much other information as is known about terrorists. Several thousand people, who belong to the staff of an organization similar to the Federal Bureau of Investigation in the United States, work on this project. This computer system is used to fight crime and terrorism, but it has been criticized by members of civil liberties groups. Many experts on terrorism reply that unless the fight against terrorism is won, there will be no civil liberties. Since democracies are targets, the question is often asked, "How much freedom should a democratic country give up in order to fight terrorism?" Is there a balance between rights of the individual and the tactics needed to deal with terrorism?

Barricades in front of vulnerable sites are another approach to prevention. Gayle Rivers suggests layered defense so that the first security barrier a terrorist would have to confront would be at a safe distance from the target. In addition to embassy guards, huge flower pots have appeared in front of some buildings. These are constructed with prestressed steel, not only in them but in the ground below, so that they could stop a vehicle as strong as a tank.

One of the major concerns of those who are working to counter terrorism is the capacity of groups to be innovative and to escalate the level of violence when they are challenged or when their acts are considered too commonplace to demand the attention they seek.

Many studies have been made on the question of whether or not terrorists will ever use nuclear weapons. It has often been noted that the first successful nuclear threat may be the last. Certainly, in such a scenario, there would be no place to hide. Sabotage of a nuclear facility or theft of a nuclear cargo are more likely to be a form of terrorist nuclear violence than the creation of a nuclear bomb from stolen material. However, the latter is not impossible.

Many experts point out that there are easier ways for terrorists to call attention to their causes than through the use of nuclear threats or actions involving radioactive material. Certain terrorists are known to have considered the use of biological weapons, such as releasing highly contagious bacteria or viruses that could ravage a continent.

Stopping shipments of money and arms that flow to terrorists, requiring new facilities to be built with more stringent security measures, increased sharing of information and extradition of offenders by free nations, stepped-up training of antiterrorist forces and increased intelligence measures are just some of the suggestions for the prevention and combating of terrorism. It has been suggested that a call for positive action on Third World grievances that have generated terrorism, strengthening international law, and a call for the end of state-sponsored terrorism should be included in counterterrorist programs. The apparent trading of arms for hostages hurt a twelve-year antiterrorist policy in the United States where complex investigations began in late 1986.

It is not the purpose of this book to attempt to answer all of the many questions about what to do about terrorism. Combating terrorism is a complex problem. But it is a problem that each person must consider as a threat to today's civilization. As terrorism persists and grows more savage, the importance of civic awareness and knowledge about the subject continues to increase. It does and will continue to play a part in everyone's life.

Suggestions for Further Reading

Adams, James. *The Financing of Terror: The PLO, IRA, Red Brigades, M-19, and Their Money Supply.* New York: Simon & Schuster, 1986

Cline, Ray S. and Yonah Alexander, *Terrorism as State-Sponsored Warfare.* Fairfax, VA: Hero Books, 1986

Clutterbuck, Richard. *Guerrillas and Terrorists.* London: Faber and Faber Ltd., 1977

Clutterbuck, Richard. *The Media and Political Violence.* London: Macmillan Press, 1981

Demaris, Ovid. *Brothers in Blood.* New York: Charles Scribner's Sons, 1977

Dobson, Christopher and Ronald Payne. *The Carlos Complex: A Study in Terror.* New York: G.P. Putnam's Sons, 1977

Dobson, Christopher and Ronald Payne. *Counterattack: The West's Battle Against the Terrorists.* New York: Facts on File, 1982

Ford, Franklin L. *Political Murder: From Tyrannicide to Terrorism.* Cambridge, MA: Harvard University Press, 1985

Hacker, Frederick J. *Crusaders, Criminals, Crazies: Terror and Terrorism in Our Time.* New York: W.W. Norton, 1976

Hippshen, Leonard J. and Yongs Yim. *Terrorism, International Crime and Arms Control.* Springfield, IL: Charles G. Thomas, 1982

Hubbard, David G. *Winning Back the Sky: A Tactical Analysis of Terrorism.* Dallas, TX: Saybrook Publishers, 1986

Kupperman, Robert and Darrell Trent. *Terrorism.* Stanford, CA: Hoover Institution Press, 1979

Liston, Robert A. *Terrorism.* Nashville, TN: Thomas Nelson, Inc., 1977

Livingston, Neil C. and Terrell E. Arnold, eds. *Fighting Back: Winning the War Against Terrorism.* Lexington, MA: Lexington Books, 1986

Melman, Yossi. *The Master Terrorist: The True Story of Abu Nidal.* New York: Adama Books, 1986

Meltzer, Milton. *The Terrorists.* New York: Harper & Row, 1983

Miller, Abraham H. *Terrorism and Hostage Negotiations.* Boulder, CO: Westview Press, 1980

Netanyahu, Benjamin, ed. *Terrorism: How the West Can Win.* New York: Farrar, Straus and Giroux, 1986

Norton, Augustus R. and Martin H. Greenberg, eds. *Studies in Nuclear Terrorism.* Boston, MA: G.K. Hall and Company, 1979

Parry, Albert. *Terrorism: From Robespierre to Arafat.* New York: The Vanguard Press, 1976

Ra'anan, Uri, Robert L. Pfaltzgraff, Jr., Richard H. Shultz, Ernst Halperin, and Igor Lukes, eds. *Hydra of Carnage: The International Linkages of Terrorism and Other Low-Intensity Operations.* Lexington, MA: Lexington Books, 1986

Rivers, Gayle. *The War Against the Terrorists: How to Win It.* New York: Stein and Day, 1986

Sterling, Claire. *The Terrorist Network.* New York: Holt, Rinehart, and Winston, 1981

Wright, Robin. *Sacred Rage: The Crusade of Modern Islam.* New York: Simon & Schuster, 1985

Index

MARGARET O. HYDE is the author of more than fifty nonfiction books for young people, many of them dealing with sensitive teenage problems. Her topics include child abuse, suicide, drug abuse, runaways, as well as science subjects. Her *Mind Drugs* is in its fifth edition. Other titles are *Sexual Abuse: Let's Talk About It; Cry Softly: The Story of Child Abuse;* and for younger readers, *Know About Smoking* and *Know About Drugs.* She has also written documentaries for NBC-TV and has served as science consultant for Lincoln School of Teachers College, Columbia University. She lives in Shelburne, Vermont.

ELIZABETH H. FORSYTH, a psychiatrist, has collaborated with Margaret O. Hyde on four previous books, including *AIDS: What Does It Mean to You?* and *Suicide: The Hidden Epidemic* (revised edition). A graduate of the Yale University School of Medicine, she has served as clinical instructor in psychiatry at University of Vermont College of Medicine, has been psychiatric consultant for the Burlington, Vermont, public school system, and currently combines private practice with forensic psychiatry. She lives in Burlington, Vermont.